Colon Classification Theory and Practice: A Self Instructional Manual

Prof. A.A.N. Raju

Former Head, Dept. of Library and Information Science

and

Dean, Faculty of Social Sciences, Osmania University,

Hyderqbad – 500 007

Ess Ess Publications

4837/24, Ansari Road, Darya Ganj,

New Delhi-110002

✆ : 3260807, 3201533

Fax: 3274173

E–mail: essess@del3.vsnl.net.in

url:http://www.essessbooks.com

First Published 2001

ISBN : 81-7000-305-9

Price : Rs.700/-

Published by :

Ess Ess Publications

4837/24, Ansari Road, Darya Ganj,
New Delhi - 110 002
Phone : 3260807
Fax: 3274173
E-mail: essess@del3.vsnl.net.in
url:http://www.essessbooks.com

Laser Typesetting :

CINOGRAPHICS
E-41, New Multan Nagar
New Delhi – 56
Ph. : 5269702

Printed at :

Print Line
New Delhi

Dedicated to

My beloved daughter

Chy. A. SRI REKHA

Who left us on 13th November, 1995
to the Heavenly abode

Contents

Preface

Colon Classification (CC) is truly the first freely faceted scheme for Library Classification designed, expounded and propagated by Dr. S.R. Ranganathan. The scheme is being taught in theory and practice to the students in almost all the Library and Information Science (LIS) schools at the postgraduate level in India and some schools abroad. In the past, many manuals, guidebooks and introductory works have been published on CC. But the present work treads a new path in presenting CC to the student, teaching and professional community.

The present work is the result of author's twenty-five years experience in teaching classification theory and practice to the students of Bachelor's Degree Programme in LIS at Osmania University, Hyderabad. The involvement of the author as Course Writer and Editor in the preparation of Course materials for BLISc/MLISc Programmes of Dr. B.R. Ambedkar Open University, Hyderabad and Indira Gandhi National Open University, New Delhi and as a Counsellor for the distance learners of BLISc/MLISc programmes of these two Open Universities, has enabled him to gain the necessary experience and expertise in presenting the thought content in self instructional mode.

Therefore an effort has been made to present CC theory and practice in self-instructional mode keeping in view the requirements of the students of conventional universities as well as distance learners of Open Universities, Distance and Correspondence Educational Institutes in the Country, which are offering LIS programmes.

The present work *Colon Classification; Theory and Practice: A Self Instructional Manual* is divided into three blocks consisting a total of twelve units. **Block-1: *Theory of Colon Classification*** consists four Units dealing with Genesis, Development and Features of CC; Time, Space and Language Isolates; Common Isolates and

System and Special. **Block-2: *Towards Coextensive Class Numbers*** consists three units. These Units deal with: Phase, Intra-facet and Intra-array relations; Different devices and Differential Facets, Parallel Schedules and Telescoped Facets. **Block-3: *Practical Classification*** consists five Units. These five Units deal with: Main Classes under Mathematical and Physical Sciences; Biological Sciences; Humanities; Social Sciences and other main classes such as Generalia Bibliography, Library Science, Useful Arts and Spiritual Experience and Mysticism.

To explain the intricacies of Colon Classification and the concepts and principles that go with theory and practice, the relevant rules from theory part have been quoted to show that construction of class number is to be done as per the rules stated in the theory part.

In Block three Practical Classification each title has been analysed and synthesized to arrive at coextensive Class Number. In the analysis part the occurrence of fundamental categories including rounds and levels of manifestation and citing the relevant isolate numbers and synthesizing them with the relevant connecting symbols to arrive at the Class Number has been attempted.

Each Unit provides necessary access devices such as: aims and objectives, introduction, section and subsection headings, self-check exercises, summary, glossary and answers to self-check exercises, to give clues to learners to comprehend the contents, retain the techniques and aspects in the memory and retrieve them when required and apply the practical skills he/she comprehends after going through this manual. The assignments provided at the end of each Unit will enable the student/distance learner to classify additional titles to acquire more practice. An effort has also been made to establish linkages between sections and subsections within a Unit and between the Units of a Block to achieve continuous flow of thought throughout so as to communicate to the learner the relevance, utility and relationship of different Units and also the theoretical and practical aspects of CC.

The Author and Publisher fervently believe that the self instructional manual on CC will go a long way in meeting the needs of students/ distance learners, teachers of LIS and also practicing librarians. Constructive and positive comments and suggestions are solicited from these groups to improve the quality of this work in the second edition. The author sincerely hopes that this manual may give an impetus to bring out such self-instructional manuals on various aspects of LIS.

Prof. A.A.N. Raju

Acknowledgments

I whole-heartedly record my sincere appreciation of the excellent work done by Sri M. Madhusudhan, my former colleague in the Department of Library and Information Science, Osmania University, who meticulously prepared the Press Copy of this work. I would be failing in my duty if I do not thank Sri Sumit Sethi, the dynamic Managing Director of Ess Ess Publications, New Delhi, who readily agreed to bring out this publication.

Sankranti **Prof. A.A.N. Raju**

14th January 2001

Hyderabad

BLOCK 1
Theory of Colon Classification (CC)

This block introduces you to the theory of Colon Classification (CC). Classification is the tool for systematic organization of knowledge/Information embodie in documents in Libraries and Information centres. Of several general schemes of Library Classification, CC is one of the prominent faceted schemes devised and propagated by S.R. Ranganathan. This block consists of the following four units (1-4) dealing with theory of CC.

Unit 1: Deals with genesis, development and features of CC. This unit also briefly touches upon the structure, layout, facet analysis and fundamental categories, rounds and levels of manifestation, notation, call number and steps in classifying a document with CC.

Unit 2 : Deals with the provision of Time, Space and Language isolates in CC and their application in the construction of Class Number. The relevant rules from CC are quoted and well supported by suitable worked out examples.

Unit 3 : Deals with provision of Common Isolates viz: Anteriorising and Posteriorinsing and their application in the construction of a Class Number. The relevant rules are quoted and well supported by worked out examples.

Unit 4. Deals with provision of System and Special which is a unique contribution to the development of theory of CC. This unit also deals with occurrence of systems and specials in some of the main classes and their use in the construction of class number citing relevant rules from theory part of CC.

UNIT 1

Genesis, Development and Features of Colon Classification

1.0 OBJECTIVES

In this Unit, we introduce you to genesis, development and features of Colon Classification (CC). After going through this Unit you should be able to:

- know the genesis and development of CC;
- familiarize the structure and layout of CC;
- understand the basic features of CC;
- grasp the concepts such as *facet analysis, fundamental categories, rounds and levels of manifestation;*
- comprehend the type of notation used in CC; and
- know the parts of Call Number

1.1 INTRODUCTION

You are aware that library classification is an important tool for classifying various types of documents acquired by Libraries and Information Centres, on the basis of subject matter or thought content embodied in documents. Library Classification helps to achieve most helpful sequence of documents on the shelves. Of several general schemes of library classification, Colon

Classification (CC) is one of the popular schemes based on sound theory. The author of this scheme is world famous classificationist Dr. S.R. Ranganathan, who devised and first published in 1933. This scheme treads a new path in mapping the universe of subjects. It stands as the best example of freely faceted scheme for classification. In this Unit we will present to you briefly biographical sketch of Ranganathan and trace the genesis, development, features and theoretical principles that are the basis for Colon Classification.

1.2 S.R. RANGANATHAN (1892-1972)

Before you are introduced to genesis, development and feature of CC, it is better to draw upon a pen picture of Dr. S.R. Ranganathan, the author and propounder of Colon Classification.

Dr. Shiyali Ramamrita Ranganathan, 'the father of Librarianship in India' was born on 9th August, 1892 at Shiyali, a village in Tanjore District of the then Madras Presidency (presently Tamilnadu). After obtaining M.A. (Maths) and L.T. Degrees from Madras University, he taught mathematics in the Government College, Madras, during the years 1917-1920. Later he became Assistant Professor of Mathematics during 1920-1923 in the Presidency College, Madras. He was appointed first full fledged Librarian of the University of Madras, without any formal library experience in 1924.

He was sent to England in 1924 for studying library methods and practices at the British Museum Library. At the suggestion of the Director of the Museum, Ranganathan joined School of Librarianship, University of London. He found only the subjects like library administration and classification very interesting. He found the lectures delivered by W.C.B. Sayers on Classification most interesting and inspiring. These lectures on classification had greater impact on Ranganathan to become later one of the most prolific authors and exponent of freely faceted scheme for library classification. His visit to Shelfridge Departmental Store in London and observance of demonstration of Meccanoset had given clue to him to design a faceted scheme for classification.

After training, Ranganathan returned to Madras with a mission to improve the library services to the people of his country. He has lost no time in putting into practice what he has observed and learnt in England. First he reorganized the Madras University Library to provide maximum service to its clientele. He started developing new scheme of Classification. He used the University Library as his laboratory to experiment and innovate new principles, techniques and methods in the field of Librarianship, especially in classification.

After retiring from University of Madras, Ranganathan spent two years (1945-46) at Banaras Hindu University as a University librarian and Professor of Library Science. Later, he was Professor at University of Delhi during the years 1947-55.In the year 1962, he established Documentation Research and Training Centre (DRTC) at Bangalore. He spent the evenings of his life at DRTC, Bangalore and passed away on 27th September 1972. Thus a glorious chapter on the history of Library Science in India has come to an end.

1.3 DIFFERENT EDITIONS OF CC

In this sub-sections we will present to you briefly different editions of CC.

First Edition, 1933

The first edition of CC was published in 1933. In its very first edition, it appeared basically different from existing schemes of classification. Each Main Class (MC) was divided on the basis of facets and each facet was provided with distinct unit schedules. Colon was used as a connecting symbol for synthesizing different facets into class number. Like enumerative classification scheme, the first edition listed 26 MCs represented by twenty-six Roman Capital letters (A-Z). Each MC has been divided on the basis trains of characteristics and shown in the facet formula provided for each MC. For example the MC Medicine has the following facet formula:

L[organ]: [Problem]: [Handling of disease]

Second Edition, 1939

The second edition did not contain any drastic changes different from the first edition (1933). On the basis of the theory enunciated by Ranganathan, certain faults found in edition 1 have been removed. Some significant features found in this edition are: 1. Schedules for common subdivisions and subjects like Sound, Electricity, Technology, Biology, Indian Philosophy, Sociology and Law have been recast. This edition consist four parts viz: Part 1: Rules of Classification, Part-2: Schedules of Classification, Part 3: Index to schedules and Part 4: Examples of Call Numbers.

Third Edition, 1950

In this edition the term 'facet' has been replaced by the phrase 'train of characteristics'. Each basic class has been provided with a facet formula on the basis of fundamental categories. Some minor changes in terminology have been incorporated. On the whole CC remained rigidly faceted classification scheme.

Fourth Edition, 1952

This edition was radically different from the previous three editions. Each fundamental category has been assigned with a distinct connecting symbol, with exception to space and time, where the same connecting symbol dot (.) was used until the sixth edition reprinted in 1963. These connecting symbols are:, comma for personality, [P],; Semicolon for Matter [M],: Colon for Energy [E],. Dot for Space [S] and Time [T]. In addition, a number of Greek alphabets were used to groups of main classes. In this edition the concept of rounds and levels were introduced.

Fifth Edition, 1957

It was proposed to bring CC into two stages from fifth edition. The version at stage 1 was intended for classifying macro documents and version at stage 2 was intended for classifying micro documents. So far version at stage 2 has not seen the light of the day.

Sixth Edition, 1960

In is edition all the Greek alphabets which were introduced

in the fourth edition (1952) with the exception of Δ Delta and Sigma Σ were replacing by introducing the concepts empty and emptying digits. It was reprinted in 1963 with certain amendments and changes. The connecting symbol (.) dot used earlier for Time has been replaced by (') single inverted comma and second level space and time isolates and common energy isolates were introduced. This edition is in three parts viz: Part 1: Rules for construction of class number, Part 2: Schedules of classification with an Index and Part 3: Schedules of classics and sacred books with special names and with an Index.

Seventh Edition, 1987

This edition was published in 1987. It was proposed to be brought out in 3 volumes, viz; Vol. I: Schedules for classification, Vol. 2 & Vol. 3 Index and worked out examples. But only Vol. I schedules for classification was published in 1987. In this edition, in addition to existing connecting symbols or indicator digits in the 6th edition (1960), few more indicator digits viz; & (ampersand), + (Plus) = (equals), * (asterisk) and ' (Single Inverted Comma) have been added. The fundamental category Matter [M] has been transformed into Matter Method [MM] and Matter Property [MP] or Matter Material [M]. This edition also provides for environmental divisions (Chapter DD). The schedules of Basic subjects have been greatly expanded. It also provides for common Matter Property Isolates. The schedules for Language, Time and Space have been greatly expanded

Self Check Exercise 1

1. In how many parts second edition of CC consists of?
2. For the first time in which edition of CC, facet formula was provided for each basic Class?
3. In which edition of CC each fundamental category was assigned distinct connecting symbols except Space and Time?
4. In which edition of CC the concept of empty and emptying digits were introduced?
5. What are the additional indicator digits introduced in the 7th edition of CC.?

1.4 STRUCTURE AND LAYOUT

In the previous sections we have introduced you to different editions of CC. In this section we will introduce you to the structure and layout of CC 6th edition. It is essential for you to know how CC 6th edition is presented. This will facilitate you to use the scheme freely for practical classification. This scheme has been divided into three parts. Part-1: Rules, Part-2: Schedules and Part-3: Schedules of classics and sacred books. Each part is briefly introduced to you for familiarization.

1.4.1 Part 1: Rules

This part deals with theoretical aspects of CC. If you peruse contents page (page-7) of this Part you will find that chapters 01 to 04 (pages 1.3 to 1.18) deal with Call Number, Class Number, Book number and Collection Number respectively. Chapters 05 to 08 (Pages 1.20 to 1.39) deal with Focus and Facet, contractions, canons of classification, principles and postulates. In these chapters i.e. 05 to 08 the theoretical basis for CC is presented with examples.

Chapters 1 to 7 (Pages 1.41 to 1.59) deal with concept of Main Class, Common Isolate, Time Isolate, Space Isolate, Language Isolate, Phase and Intra-Facet Relations and Classic. In these chapters you will also find worked out examples which will help you in practical classification.

Chapters 9z to Z (pages 1.62 to 1.121) deal with rules and worked out examples pertaining to different main classes starting with Generalia and ending with Law. At the end of Part-1, there is and Index (Page 1.123). To sum up Part-1 presents the theoretical basis of CC and provides guidelines for the use of schedules in Part-2 for the construction of class numbers

1.4.2 Part-2: Schedules of Classification

This part provides schedules of classification for different main classes listed at Chapter-1 (Page 2.4). Besides these schedules, this part provides schedules for Book Number (page 2.3), Common Isolate (Page 2.5), Time Isolate (Page 2.7), Space Isolate (Page 2.8), Language Isolate (Page 2.26)and Phase and Intra-Facet and Intra array relations (Page 2.28). The schedules for different Main

Classes from Zeneralia to Law are presented between Pages 2.29 to 2.123. At the end of Part-2, there is Index to Schedules (Pages 2.124 to 2.172).

In addition to general index to schedules at Page 1.124, there are special alphabetical indexes to the Space Isolates (Page 2.18) and of Personality Isolates in Botany (Page 2.61) and Zoology (Page 2.73). These indexes help us to locate a particular isolate of place or plant or an animal in the respective schedules.

1.4.2.1 Main Classes in CC

The following is the list of Main Class (MCs) we find at Part-2, Chapter 1, Page 2.4

Z	Generalia
1	Universe of Knowledge
2	Library Science
3	Book Science
4	Journalism
A	Natural Sciences
AZ	Mathematical Sciences
B	Mathematics
BZ	Physical Sciences
C	Physics
D	Engineering
E	Chemistry
F	Technology
G	Biology
HX	Mining
I	Botany
J	Agriculture
K	Zoology
KX	Animal Husbandry
L	Medicine
LX	Pharmacognosy

H	Useful Arts
Δ	Spiritual Experience and Mysticism
MZ	Humanities and social Sciences
MZA	Humanities
N	Fine Arts
NX	Literature and Language
O	Literature
P	Linguistics
Q	Religion
R	Philosophy
S	Psychology
Σ	Social Sciences
T	Education
U	Geography
W	Political Science
X	Economics
Y	Sociology
YX	Social Work
Z	Law

The Classes B to M are all sub-divisions of Class A Natural Sciences. The Classes E to F constitutes the generic class called "Physical Sciences''. The classes G to L constitute generic Class called "Bio-sciences''. The Classes T to Z constitute the generic class called "Social Sciences''. This is represented by the Greek Letter Σ (Sigma). The Classes N to S constitute the generic class called "Humanities''. This is represented by MZA.

1.4.2.2 Canonical Classes

Canonical Class means traditional subdivision of a main class enumerated as such in scheme of classification for the Universe of Knowledge and not derived on definite characteristics. Some of the Main Classes viz. B Mathematics, C Physics, H Geology, M Useful Arts, N Fine Arts, and R Philosophy are divided in the first instance into Canonical Classes.

1.4.3 Schedules of Classics and Sacred Books

This part provides workedout depth class numbers by applying classic device for classics in Indology. It also includes schedules of sacred books with special names. This part is very useful to those Libraries and Information Centres specialized in Indological Collections. Classics dealing with L Medicine is presented at Page 3.3; Δ Spiritual Experience and Mysticism, at Page 3.3; N Fine Arts at page 3.7; O Literature at Page 3.8; P Linguistics at Page 3.14; Q religion at Page 3.22 and R Philosophy at Page 3.34. There is an index for classics and sacred books at Page 3.54.

1.4.4 Annexure to Edition 6

The reprint of Edition 6 (1960) published in 1963, provides an Annexure incorporating major changes brought into use after 1960. This contains also corrections of miss-prints and few minor changes. This is inserted at the end of preliminary pages i.e. after Page 16, but before the title page of Part-1. You have to be familiarize with this annexure while using the schedules dealing with physical features, population clusters orientation divisions, revised schedule for M7 Textiles and V: 19 Foreign Policy.

1.4.5 Pagination

We will not find continuous pagination in CC. Each part has a different pagination. We have to keep this fact in mind. The page number for each part is represented by two blocks and are separated by a .dot. The number appearing to the left of the .dot indicates part number and the number to the right of the .dot indicates page numbers in that part. Take for example 1.24 means page 24 in Part-1; 2.40 means page 40 in Part-2 and 3.51 means Page 51 in Part-3.

Self Check Exercise:2

(a) What are the chapters 9z to Z in Part-1 deal with?

(b) Identify the page numbers for Common Isolates, Time Isolates, Phase, Intra Facet and Intra-array relations from Part-2.

(c) Which part of CC is useful for classifying books on Indological subjects.

1.5 Facet Analysis and Fundamental Categories

CC is one of the best freely faceted general schemes of classification. It is primarily based on the concept of facet analysis and fundamental categories. Facet analysis means analysis of a subject into facets according to the postulates and principles stated for the purpose. Facet means generic name for a basic class or an isolate or a subject. Fundamental Categories means generic terms denoting Time, Space, Energy, Matter and Personality. These are only postulated categories.

1.5.1 Facet analysis

In CC some of the Main Classes such as B Mathematics, C Physics, H Geology, M useful Arts, N Fine Arts and R Philosophy are divided in the first instance into canonical classes or traditional divisions of a subject. Each Main Class or Canonical Class is said to be a Basic Class (BC). Basic Class means generic name for a main class or cononical class.

Each basic class may be divided on the basis of one or more trains of characteristics. Characteristic means an attribute or complex of attributes. Trains of Characteristics means applying more than one characteristic to divide a basic subject. Let us take for example Basic Class Literature, which admits of four trains of characteristics. These are Language, Form, Author and work of an author. In this (BC), we may identify four facets; the Language, the Form, the Author and the work. When a title is given to us for classification first we have to identify the specific subject of the document and to which Basic Class (BC), the subject belongs. After identifying the (BC) we have to recognize the facets, which the specific subject admits. This analysis of facets in a given specific subject is called facet analysis.

In the above Basic Class (BC) Literature we have identified four facets which are identified by the symbols [P], [P2], [P3] and P4 respectively. The facet formula given for Main Class (MC) literature in Part-2: Schedules of CC (Page 2.94) is as follows. [P],

[P2], [P3], [P4]. This facet formula can be written with the following words: O [Languages], [Form] [Author], and [Work]. This is the sequence of facets in CC for construction of class number. Out of twenty-four ways of arranging the above four facets, the above sequence suggested in the facet formula by S.R. Ranganathan found to be most helpful.

Let us take another example of facet analysis. The (BC) Linguistics admits of four trains of characteristics: Language, Variant and Stage, Element and Problem. In the subject of (BC)Linguistics we may recognize four facets viz. Language, Variant and Stage, Element and Problem. The four facets are indicated by the symbols [P] [P2] [P3] and [E] respectively. The facet formula given in the schedules for Linguistics Basic Class at Page 2.95 is:

P[P], [P2], [P3]:[E] [2P]

The above facet formula can be written in the following words.

P[Language], [Variant and stage][Element]. The facet formula prescribes the sequence in which the four facets should be arranged in the class number. For more information read Chapter 05 Page 1.20

1.5.1.1 Facets and Isolates

In each facet formula, each square bracket represents a single train of characteristics. The totality of the divisions of a (BC) based on a single train of characteristics is said to constitute one of its facets. In the above example from the Main Class Linguistics, Language, Variant and Stage, Element and Problem are facets. Each division of a facet is said to be an Isolate. It is generic term to denote isolate idea (Idea Plane) or isolate term (Verbal Plane) or isolate number (Notational Plane). For example in the Main Class Linguistics, the language facet consists a number of language isolates such as English, German, Sanskrit, Hindi, Telugu and so on. Please refer Chapter 5 Part 1, Page 1.20 for more information.

1.5.2 Fundamental Categories

After analysis of the facets in a given subject, the next step is to transform them into fundamental categories. According to Ranganathan "there are five and only five fundamental categories viz. Personality, Matter, Energy, Space and Time''. Each facet of any subject, as well as each focus (Isolate) in it is regarded as a manifestation of one of the five fundamental categories (FFC). The FFC are given below in the increasing sequence of concreteness with respective connecting symbols.

Fundamental Category (FC)	Connecting Symbol (CS)	Symbol for the Facet
Time	' (Single Quote Mark)	[T]
Space	. (Dot)	[S]
Energy	: (Colon)	[E]
Matter	; (Semi Colon)	[M]
Personality	, (Comma)	[P]

In the class number each fundamental category is represented by its prescribed connecting symbol unless its omission is indicated by Facet Formula or by Rule. The first personality isolate number of any Basic Class need not be preceded by Comma. In case of amplified facets i.e. system and special, personality isolate number is to be preceded by comma. The connotation of these five terms is explained in the following subsections.

1.5.2.1 Time

Perhaps the fundamental category Time is easy to recognize in any specific subject. It means absolute duration, a moment at which things happen. It manifests in the form of different functions like century, year, month, day, hour or different seasons like winter, summer, autumn or day time, night, dry period, etc. In CC at Page 2.7 i.e. Part-2 at Chapter 3, you will find time isolates T1 and T2. Any subject is qualified by time. Take for example (1) History of India up to 1947, (2) Social conditions of India during 20th Century, (3) Winter Games. In these three titles, *1947, 20th century and winter*, is the manifestation of the fundamental category 'Time'.

1.5.2.2 Space

The second fundamental category, which can be easily recognized is space. Space means that which material bodies have extension. Space usually manifests itself as a geographical area. It manifests in the form world, countries, states, towns, villages, zones like, equatorial, tropical, orientation divisions like East, West, North, South, physiographical features like, mountain, river, valley etc. Chapter-4: Part-2 (page 2.8) deals with Geographical Isolates (S1) and Physiographical isolates (S2). Like Time, Space also qualifies almost every subject. Take for example titles like; (1) Higher education in UK, (2) Living Conditions in Mumbai, (3) Holy places in the Himalayas. In these three titles UK, Mumbai and Himalayas is the manifestation of fundamental category 'Space'

1.5.2.3 Energy

Fundamental Category Energy is very dominant facet in CC. It means power of doing work, vigorous activity of one kind or another. It manifests in the form of activities, processes, operations, problems etc. For examples activities like cataloging, operations like, sowing, transplanting, harvesting and problems like crime, pathology, disease, alcoholism and many more are the manifestation of fundamental category Energy. Take for example titles like 1. Documentation in India, 2. Tropical diseases, 3. University examinations, 4. Accidents in coal mines. In these four titles the isolates documentation, diseases, examinations and accidents are manifestation of the fundamental Category 'Energy'.

1.5.2.4 Matter

The fundamental category matter means that which occupies space or with which we become acquainted with bodily sense. It manifests as material or any equivalent of it. It is not difficult to recognize it in any specific subject. In CC, Matter facet does not occur in many of the Main classes. It appears as reading materials like book, periodical, thesis, film roll, etc. in Library Science, materials used for painting such as wood, paper, stone, metal, canvas. etc. in main class for Painting and as gold, silver, paper in money in Economics. Let us take examples like, 1. Circulation of periodicals, 2. Paper Currency, 3. Canvas painting. In these three titles, Periodicals, Paper and Canvas are the manifestation of the fundamental category 'Matter'.

4.5.2.4 Personality

The last of the five fundamental categories is Personality. It is rather difficult concept to define. Ranganathan has not defined Personality. He suggested that it is often only recognizable by elimination form given specific subject. After separating out manifestation of Time, Space, Energy and Matter in a subject the residue will often turn out to be Personality, by the process of elimination. This may be called method of residue. Let us take for example titles like Reference Service in Public Libraries, Circulation of blood, 3. Rigvedic Scriptures, 4. Urban Sociology, and 5. Management of Commercial Bank. In these five titles Public Libraries, Blood, Rigvedic, Urban and Commercial Bank are manifestation of Personality facet.

While constructing the class number the five fundamental categories fall into following sequences when arranged according to their decreasing concreteness P, M, E, S, T. This is according to Ranganathan's postulate of concreteness. Like wise while constructing the class number for a specific subject the basic fact of the subject should be put first and facets should be arranged thereafter in the sequence of decreasing concreness i.e. (BC) [P]; [M]: [E]. [S] '[T]. Please refer section 053 part 1, P1-25 for more examples.

Self Check Exercise 3:

(a) Write the facet formula given for Main Class 'Literature'

(b) What are the Five Fundamental Categories?

(c) Write connecting symbols of Personality, Energy and Time.

1.6 ROUNDS AND LEVELS OF MANIFESTATION

It is possible that in a given specific subject we may find more than five or less than five facets. The facets may be manifestation of one fundamental category or all the five fundamental categories. Such type of manifestations according to Ranganathan is called Rounds of manifestation and Levels of manifestation. By expounding these two concepts Ranganathan limited the number of fundamental categories only to five. To support these two concepts he has enunciated certain postulates. The relevant postulates are cited in the succeeding subsections with suitable examples.

1.6.1 Rounds of Manifestation

According to Ranganathan 'Energy' may manifest itself in one and the same subject more than once. The second, third etc. manifestations of Energy in one and the same subject, are called 'Second Round Energy' [2E], 'Third Round Energy' [3E] etc. The first manifestation may be called First Round Energy i.e. simply [E] instead of [1E].

It is possible for manifestation of Personality and Matter to occur after first round Energy. These manifestations are respectively called Second Round Matter [2M]. It is possible for manifestation of Personality and Matter to occur after Second Round Energy. These manifestations are respectively called Third Round Personality [3P] and Third Round Matter [3M]. This phenomenon of Rounds of manifestation is demonstrated by this example.

Radium treatment of brain tumor in India brought up to 1990s.

First we have to identify the Basic Class to which this title belongs. We have to make the title more explicit. The full name of the subject is "treatment of disease of brain by radium caused by tumor in Medicine in India brought up to 1990s''. This is called expressed title. The next step is to identify the manifestation of fundamental categories. As stated already Personality is the most elusive one. There we have to follow the method of residue to identify Personality. Let us identify the remaining four fundamental categories i.e. [T],[S], [E], and [M].

In the above title:

Brought up to 1990s is manifestation of time i.e. 'Time Isolate'

India is manifestation of Space i.e. 'Space Isolate'.

Now we have to find out manifestation of Energy. There are two energy isolates viz.:1. Treatment, and 2. Disease. There is no manifestation of Matter. The word groups, still left are 1) Radium; 2) Brain 3) Tumor, and 4) Medicine. Of these, Medicine is the (BC). We have left with three word groups to be identified. None of them is a manifestation of Time or Space or Energy or Matter. Therefore they must be manifestation of Personality. As a result of this facet analysis we can rewrite the above subject as follows:

"Radium [P], treatment [E], of the disease [E], of brain [P], caused by tumor [P], in Medicine [BC], in India [S] brought up to 1990s [T]''. The class number for the above title is: L 72 : 472 : 63129.44'N9.

Analysis of the Class Number:

L	Medicine [BC]
72	Brain [P]
4	Disease [E] i.e. [1E]
72	Tumor [P] i.e. [2P]
6	Treatment [E] i.e. [2E]
3129	Radium [P] i.e. [3P]
44	India [S] i.e. [S1]
1990s	Time [T] i.e. [T1]

Ordinarily 'space' and 'time' should be put last in the sequence in which they are stated in the expressive title

1.6.1 Levels of manifestation

Like Rounds of Manifestation, Ranganathan postulated Levels of Manifestation in respect of fundamental categories P, M, S and T. According to him Personality may manifest in one and the same round in a subject more than once i.e. two or more levels. So also in the case of Matter, Space and Time. The second, third, etc. manifestations of Personality and Matter are called Second level Personality [P2]. Third level Personality [P3], Second level Matter [M2] and so on. The second and third level manifestations of Space and Time are represented by [S2], [S3], and [T2] and [T3]. The phenomena is demonstrated by the following example:

"Criticism of Gitanjali''. The title is not very explicit. We have to make it expressive title by providing absent concepts. The [BC] is Literature. "Criticism of Gitanjali of Rabindranath Tagore, the poet in the literature of Bengali Language.

In the above expressive the title there is no [T] or [S] or [M]. Criticism is [E] . The facet analysis of the full name of the subject is "Criticism [E] of Gitanjali [P] of Tagore [P], the Poet [P], in the literature [BC] of Bengali Language [P]. After the analysis, we got one [E] and four [P]. This is a new phenomenon where [P] manifests in one of the same round more than once in the form of levels. How to decide the sequence of these five facets. We have to reason as follows:

'Criticism' presupposes the work criticized. Therefore, we have to agree that 'Criticism' should come only after [P] Gitanjali. Likewise, "Gitanjali'' presupposes 'Tagore', Tagore presupposes 'Poetry' and poetry presupposes 'Bengali Language'. Therefore, the sequence of facets is as follows:

Literature	English	Poetry	Tagore	Gitanjali	Criticism
(BC)	[P]	[P]	[P]	[P]	[E]

Here [P] occurs four times in the first round itself. The levels of [P] in the first round may represented by [1P1], [1P2], [1P3], and [1P4]. The facet [E] is common energy facet. The Class Number for the above subject is 0157, 1M61, 1:g. In this Class Number the connecting symbol, (Comma) between number 1 and M61 is omitted as per the postulate "Omission of connecting symbol''.

Please refer section of 056 and 057 Part-1, Page 1.27 to Page 1.128 for examples.

Analysis of the Class Number:

O = Literature (MC)

157 = Bengali Language [1P1] represents language of the work

1 = Poetry [1P2] form of the work

M61 = Tagore [1P3] got by chronological Device. Author of the work

I = Gitanjali [1P4] work No.

g = Criticism [E] Common Energy Isolate.

Self Check Exercise-4:

(a) Which are the fundamental categories manifest themselves in one and the same round more than once.

(b) Identify the rounds of manifestations of fundamental categories in the following title:

"Treatment of TB of Lungs by x-ray therapy".

(c) Which are the fundamental categories manifest in the form of levels.

(d) Identify the levels of manifestation of fundamental category in the given Title: Tolstoy: War and Peace.

1.7 NOTATION

Notation means the system of ordinal numbers representing classes in a scheme of library classification. The notation in CC is mixed one that is a variety of symbols are used to main classes, fundamental categories, devices etc. The following is the type of symbols used in CC.

S.No.	*Type of digits*	*No. of digits used*
1.	Indo Arabic numerals (1/9)	9
2.	Roman alphabets: Capital letters (A/Z)	26
3.	Roman alphabets Small letters or Italics (excluding i,*l*,o)	23
4.	Greek alphabets Δ Delta, Σ Sigma.	2
5.	Parenthesis ( ) (Starter,) arrester	2
6.	Punctuation Marks to represent Fundamental categories:	5
	Inverted Comma	
	Dot	

	Colon	:	
	Semi Colon	;	
	Comma	,	
	Hyphen	-	1
7.	Zero as a connecting symbol		1
8.	Arrows:		
	Forward Arrow →		1
	Backward Arrow ←		1

The symbols Indo-Arabic numerals (1/9) and Roman Capitals are used to represent various Basic or Main Classes. Roman smalls are used to represent a variety of Common Isolates. Parenthesis is used to indicate subject Device (SD). The Punctuation marks are used to indicate the Five Fundamental Categories (FFC). The symbol-hyphen is used to represent Super Imposition Device (SID). The digit O (zero) is used to indicate Phase, Intra-Facet and Intro-Array relations. Forward and Backward arrows are used to indicate different span of time and future and past. Please refer Chapter 02 (page 1.5) of CC for detailed explanation of the symbols used in CC.

SELF CHECK EXERCISE-5:

(a) What type of notation is used in CC.

(b) For what purpose Roman small letters are used in CC.

(c) For what purpose the symbols-(hyphen),( ) parenthesis and O Zero is used in CC.

1.8 CALL NUMBER

After familirising with the type of notation used in CC now let us understand what is meant by Call Number. It means an ordinal number which fixes the position of a book/document in a library. In libraries the user community use the 'call number' to call for a book. It consists of three parts viz. Class number, Book Number and Collection Number. These three components can be written horizontally or vertically. Let us understand the three components briefly.

1.8.1 Class Number

Class Number of a book is the translation of the name of its specific subject into artificial language of ordinal numbers. It becomes the symbol used to fix the position of its specific subject relatively to other subjects. In CC it consists of ten Indo-Arabic numerals, Twenty six Roman Capital letters and Twenty three Roman small letter (except i, *l*, o) some Greek Alphabets, Punctuation marks, circular brackets and two arrows. By using colon classification schedule (Part 2) we get the class number for specific subject of a book.

1.8.2 Book Number

Book Number means ordinal number which fixes the position of a document in a library relative to other documents having same ultimate class. It is the translation of the names of certain of its specific features other than thought content into artificial languages of ordinal numbers.

1.8.2.1 Colon Scheme of Book Number

Colon Classification is one of the few schemes which provides for a scheme of book numbers in part 2 of schedules (Chapter 0.2, P. 2.3). This facet formula consists of eight facets. These eight facets are briefly explained with examples.

[L] [F] [Y] [A].[V]-[S];[C]:[Cr]

L = Language Number

F = Form Number (To be taken from chapter 0.2 Part 2 of CC)

Y = Year Number

A = Accession part of book number

V = Volume Number

S = Supplement Number

C = Copy Number

Cr = Criticism Number

The above facets are explained with examples.

L= Language: Language number is to be got by translating the name of the language in which book is written into appropriate symbols. The language number is to be taken from language isolates in chapter 5, part 2.26.If the library collection is in favoured language of the library there is no need to use language number. Except for translations in literature (O) and languages (P), this facet is rarely used.

Eg: Shakespear's Hamlet translated into Telugu by L.K. Mohan, published in 1960.

0111, 2J64, 1

Telugu ← 35 Ko → Year of publication taken from special chronological table for book Number, chapter 1, P.1.13.

F = Form Number. It is to be got by translating the name of the form of exposition into appropriate symbols in accordance with the Form Schedule in Part-2 Chapter 02, page 2.3.

Eg. Indian Philosophy in verse form

R6

w1

Saivism in dialogue form

Q23

p2

Y = Year Number: It is to be got by translating the number of the year of publication into appropriate symbols in accordance with the time schedule given Part 2, Chapter 3, P2.7 of the schedules. Libraries can also use special chronological schedule provided in CC in part 1. Chapter 03, P 1.13.

Eg: Colon Classification 6th Edn. Published in 1960.

According to 2:51N3 Time Isolates N60 At Page 2.7	OR	2:51N3 According to K0 Special Chronological Table at page 1.3.

A = Accession part of book number: When the above rules give the same book number to two or more books having the same class number these should be arranged in the sequence of accession number. In the case of the first book, the book number should end with the year number. In the case of the second, the digit 1 should be added after the year number.

Eg: Economic conditions of India 1998.

First book	X.44 N8
Second book	X.44 N81
Fifth book	X.44 N84
Tenth book	X.44 N89 and so on.

V = Volume Number: A book may appear in more than one volume. In such cases all the volumes of a multi volumed book should be brought together. If each volume treats distinct subject they can be separated.

Eg: V1 Political Science

V2 Economics

V3 Public Administration and so on.

But a set is seemed to be indivisible and to form a multi volumed book if one of the following conditions hold good. 1. The set possess a common Index, 2. The same sequence of page nation continues and 3. The subject is so distributed among the volumes of the set it is not desirable to treat each volume a separate book.

Eg: Encyclopedia of Music, 1962 6 volumes.

NRK K2.1	Volume 1
NRK K2.2	Volume 2
NRK K2.3	Volume 3 and so on.

Some times all the volumes of a indivisible set are not published in the same year and according to serial order. In such cases the year of publication of an indivisible set is the year in which the earliest published volume of the set is published.

Eg: Encyclopedia of Music 6 volumes.

NR*K*

K2.2 V2 Published in 1962.

NR*K*

K2.1 V1 Published in 1963

NR*K*

K2.3, V3 Published in 1964, and so on.

S = Supplement Number: To up date the volumes of a multi volumed book supplements are published. In such cases the Book Number (s) of the supplementary volumes (s) should consist of the Book Number of corresponding main volume followed by – dash which is, itself followed by the number of supplement in Indo-Arabic numerals.

Encyclopedia of Music. 1962, 6 vols.

NR*K*

K2.2-1 Supplement 1 to Volume 2.

NR*K*

K2.2.-2 Supplement 2 to Volume 2.

NR*K*

K2.2-3 Supplement 3 to Volume 2.

C = Copy Number: In libraries we find for some books with multiple copies to meet the demands of user community. In such cases all the copies of a particular book should come together on the shelves. The Book Number of second, third, etc., copies of a book should consists that of the first copy followed by a ; semi colon and thereafter by the digits 1,2,3, etc. respectively.

Eg: Colon Classification 6th Edition 1960

2:51N3

K0 First Copy

2:51N3

K0;1 Second Copy

2:51N3

K0;9 Tenth Copy and so on.

Cr = Criticism Number : If a particular book does not fall under Classic but another book is written on it for example evaluation, criticism or reply, then it is better to keep the criticism book along with the original book. The former is called to Host Book and the later is called Associated Book. Thee book number of associated book should consist that of host book followed by ":g"

Eg: Constitution of India. 1950

V44;2

JO

Commentary on the Constitution of India 1951

V44:2

JO:g

Accession part of the Criticism Number

This facet is not shown in the fact formula. But for certain host books we may find more than one evaluation or criticism. In such cases the book number of second, third, etc. associated books of the same host book should consist of that of the first followed by the digits 2,3, etc. respectively

Eg: Commentary on the Constitution of India. 1962 (second Commentary)

V44:2

JO:g1 Second Commentary

V44:2

JO:g2 Third Commentary

V44:2

JO:g9 Tenth Commentary, and so on.

For detailed exposition of Book Number, refer to chapter 03 of Part-1 Page 1.9

1.8.3 Collection number

This is third part of the call number. The collection number of a book denotes collection to which it belongs. Each library can devise its own collection number depending upon its collection and requirements. Ranganathan has provided the following scheme of collection number. See Chapter 04, Part 1, Page 1.18

Collection (Physical Aspects)	*Collection Number*	*Example*
Under sized	Underline Book Number	V44:2 KO
Over Sized	Over line the Book Number	V44.2 KO
Abnormal	Underline and over line Book Number	V44.2 KO
Worn-out	Encircle the Book Number	V44.2 (KO)

Collection (Types)	*Collection Number*
Reading Room	RR
Rare Book	RB
Text Book	TB
Reference Department	RD
Theses and Dissertation	TD

1.8.4 Method of writing call number

The three parts of the call number should be written quite distinct from one another. There are two methods of writing three parts. These can be written in horizontal straight line having sufficient but uniform space between the parts.

Eg: V44:2 KO RR-Reading room

These three parts also can be written vertically one below the other.

Eg: V44:2 -Class number
KO -Book number
RR -Collection number.

Self Check Exercise 6:

(A) Name the three parts of call number

(B) What is meant by Book Number

(C) How many facets are there in Ranganathan's facet formula for Book Number

(D) How to indicate wornout book in the Book Number

1.9 STEPS IN CLASSIFYING DOCUMENTS

Ranganathan identified eight steps for classifying a document. These steps are explained in chapter 02, Part 1, Page 1.7

Step 0: Raw title = Title found in the document

Step 1: Full title = Title expressing each of the relevant basic isolate ideas.

Step 2: Kernal title = Full title minus auxiliary words.

Step 3: Analysed title = Kernal title with each Kernal term marked by a symbol denoting Fundamental category.

Step 4: Transformed title = Analysed title with Kernal terms rearranged according to Symbols of analysis.

Step 5: Title in standard terms = Kernal terms replaced by their respective equivalents as give in the schedules.

Step 6: Title in facet numbers = Kernal terms replaced by their equivalent numbers

Step 7: Class number got by removing the symbols of analysis and inserting the appropriate connecting symbols between Facet numbers according to rules.

Example

Step0: *Raw title*: Problems of management of steel industry in India in 1990s

Step 1: *Full title*: Problems of managing steel industry (in economics) in India 1990s

Step 2: *Kernal title*: Management, Steel industry, Economics, India, 1990s

Step 3: *Analysed title*: Management (E), Steel Industry (P), Economics (BC). India (S), 1990s (T).

Step 4: *Transformed title*: Economics (BC), Steel Industry (P), Management (E) India (S), 1990s (T).

Step 5: *Title in standard terms*: Economics (BC), Steel Industry (P), Management (E), India (S), 1990s (T).

Step 6: *Title in focal numbers* : X (BC) 8 (F 1823) [P] 8 [E] 44 [S] N9 [T]

Step 7: *Class number X8 (F1823)*: 8.44 n9

Note: The number for steel 1823 is not given the schedules of Economics under (P), See Part 1, P 1.77 for worked out examples under chapter f. Technology.

1.10. INDEX TO SCHEDULES

As we told you in section 1.4, alphabetical index to schedules is provided in CC at page 2.124. This is an index to fundamental constituent terms in the schedules of classification. This index provides us to identify the Basic class and the facets with isolate numbers for a specific subject. At the beginning of the index; you will find contractions used in the index and interpretation of entries taken out from the index. You have to understand the implications of each entry given in the index. From this index we may get ready made class number, but on the basis facets and isolates numbers indicated in each entry and you have to synthesise class number. Here is an example:

Esophagus has isolate number 23 in personality of G, Biology, Second level personality facet in K Zoology and personality facet in L Medicine.

Therefore class member is

G23

K, 23

L 23

Self Check Exercise 7

A. What is meant by Kernal title.

B. What is meant by title in standard terms.

C. What is the nature of index to schedules.

D. Find out the class number for "Transformers', 'Artificial boundary' 'Correspondence course' with the help of index.

1.11 OTHER FEATURES OF CC

CC provides for a variety of common isolates, space and time isolates which act as auxiliaries for the construction of class number. In addition, the scheme also provides for systems and specials, phase relations, telescoping of facets, mnemonics and a variety of devices which help to achieve coextensive class number. These features are presented to you in the succeeding units.

1.12.1 Summary

The author of Colon Classification is S.R. Ranganathan, who brought first edition in 1933. Later six more editions were published culminating the publication of seventh edition in 1987. CC is presented in three parts. Part-1: Rules, Part-2: Schedules of Classification ad Part-3: Schedules of Classics and Sacred Books. CC is primarily based on the concept of facet analysis and fundamental categories. Fundamental categories are generic terms denoting Time, Space, Energy, Matter and Personality.

Ranganathan postulated that in a given specific subject we find more than five or less than five facets. These facets may be the manifestation of one or all the five fundamental categories. Such manifestation of fundamental categories, according to Ranganathan is Rounds of Manifestation and Level of Manifestation.

The notation is mixed one consisting of Indo-Arabic numerals, Roman capital letters and Roman small letters, Greek alphabets, punctuation marks and symbols. Each species is used for specific purpose. The purpose of classification is to achieve Call number which consists of three parts viz: Class Number, Book

Number and Collection Number. Ranganathan advocated eight step method for construction of a class number. The Index to Schedules provided at the end of Part 2 is a tool to use the schedules and identify the main class (es), the relevant facets and isolate number for specific subject and to derive the class number from each entry. There are other important feature such as Common Isolate, Space Isolate, Time Isolate, Systems and Specials, Phase Relations which are presented in succeeding Units.

1.13 KEY WORDS

Basic Class

Generic name for a main or canonical class.

Book Number

Ordinal number which fixes the position of a document in a library relative to other documents having the ultimate class.

Call Number

Ordinal number which fixes the position of a document in a library.

Canonical Class

Traditional sub-class of a main class.

Collection Number

Symbol to denote collection other than the main.

Facet

Generic name for a basic class or an isolate of a subject.

Facet Analysis

A Analysis of a subject in to facets according to postulates and principles.

Faceted Classification

A scheme of classification involving analysis of a subject into facets and synthesizing the class number with the help of basic focus and isolate numbers.

Fundamental Categories

Generic term denoting time, space, energy, matter and personality.

Isolate (idea)

Thought unit which is usually a manifestation of one of the five fundametnal categories.

Levels of manifestation: Manifestation or appearance of Personality and Matter more than once in each round.

Main Class

Class enumerated in the array of order 1, in a scheme of classification for the Universe of knowledge.

Notation

The system of Ordinal numbers representing the classes in a scheme of classification.

Rounds of manifestation

Manifestation or appearance of Energy in one and the same subject more than once. So also Personality and Matter may manifest after first round of Energy.

1.14 ANSWERS TO SELF CHECK EXERCISES

Exercise-1

(a) Four parts, viz. 1 Rules, 2. Schedules of Classification, 3. Index to schedules and 4. Examples of Call Numbers.

(b) Third Edition (1950)

(c) Fourth Edition (1952)

(d) Sixth Edition (1960)

(e) & (ampersand) + (Plus), = (equals), *(asterisk), and '(Single inverted comma)

Exercise-2

(a) Rules and worked out examples pertaining to different main classes.

(b) Page 2.5, Page 2.7. Page 2.8.

(c) Part 3 of CC

Exercise-3

(a) 0[P], [P2], [P3], [P4]

(b) Personality, Matter, Energy, Space and Time

(c) , (Comma), : (Colon), '(Single quote mark)

Exercise-4

(a) Energy, Personality and Matter

(b) Medicine (MC), Lungs [P], Disease [E], T.B. [P], Treatment [E], X-Ray[P].

(c) Personality, Matter, Space and time.

(d) Literature (MC), Russian Language [P], Fiction [P], Tolstoy [P], War and Peace [P] (Work No.)

Exercise-5

(a) Mixed notation

(b) To represent Common Isolates

(c) 'Super Imposition' device, subject device and to indicate phase relations.

Exercise-6

(a) Class Number, Book Number and Collection Number

(b) The ordinal number which fixes the position of the document relative to other document having the same ultimate class.

(c) Eight Facets,

(d) By encircling the Book Number.

Exercise-7

(a) Title derived from full title by removing all the Auxiliary terms and puffs.

(b) Kernal terms replaced by their respective equivalents as given in the Schedules.

(c) It is an Index to fundamental constituent terms in the schedules of classification.

(d) D66, 14;Z, 2, 9391; T: 4, 8

1.15 ASSIGNMENT

1. Identify the Basic Class or Main Class for the following subjects:

   (a) Reference service in Libraries

(b) Theory of equation
(c) Crystallography
(d) Rice harvesting
(e) Bhakti Yoga
(f) Teaching technique
(g) India's foreign policy

2. Identify the Main Class and Facets in the following titles:
   (a) Bibliography of manuscripts
   (b) Administration of College Libraries
   (c) Propagation of Sound
   (d) Foundation of building
   (e) Drainage in Coal mines
   (f) Models of Indian architecture
   (g) Telugu Syntax
   (h) Artbitration in Iron Industry
3. Find out the relevant sections for the following aspects from Part-1 of CC.
   (a) Raw title
   (b) Notation
   (c) Basic Class
   (d) Fundamental Categories
   (e) Classic device
   (f) Seminal mnemonics
   (g) Chronological device
   (h) Phase relation
4. Apply the eight step method for arriving at the Class Number for the following titles:

(a) Designs of Railway Carriages
(b) Qualitative analysis of salt
(c) Prevention of accidents in coal mines in India during 1990s
(d) Earth Quake relief work in Peru in 1998.

1.16 SUGGESTED READINGS

1. Raju, A.A.N. 1984. *Decimal, Universal Decimal and Colon Classification*. Ajanta Publications, Delhi.
2. Ranganathan, S.R. 1962. *Elements of Library Classification*. 3rd Edn. Asia Publishing House, Bombay.
3. ———————————— 1969, *Colon Classification*. 6th Edn. Reprint: Asia Publishing House, Bombay.

UNIT 2

Time, Space and Language Isolates

0 Objectives 1 Introduction 2 Time Isolate 3 Space Isolate 4 Language Isolate 5 Summary 6 Key Words 7 Answer to Self-Check Exercises 8 Assignment 9 Suggested Readings

2.0 OBJECTIVES

In unit 1, you have been introduced to important features of colon classification. In this unit you will be introduced in the treatment of Time, Space and Language isolates in C.C. After going the rough this unit you will able to:

- Understand and use of various aspects of Time isolate such as chronological and featured time isolates.
- Apply various aspects of Space isolate such as zone, orientation, physical feature and population cluster., and
- Use of Language isolates in literature and linguistics and coin numbers for other languages not listed and newly emerging artificial languages.

2.1 INTRODUCTION

Chapters 3, 4 & 5 of CC part 1 deal with various aspects of Time, Space and Language Isolates. The schedules for Time, Space and Language are given chapters 3 (P 2.7), 4 (P 2.8to 2.17) and 5 (P 2.26 to 2.27). As explained to you in Unit 1. Subsections 1.5.2.1 and 1.5.2.2 Time and Space are two of the five fundamental categories, which are common to almost all the basic classes and main classes. Therefore these two are common facets. Any subject is qualified by space and time. The schedules time space become common schedules, which were listed at place. These can be used for any specific subject qualified by space and time.

Language isolates are also common for the main classes O Literature and P Linguistics. These also can be used to represent language facet in the book number. In addition, in the personality facet of the (MC) Generation Bibliography, isolates 2 (By script) and 3 (By language) is to be divided by language. To a larger extent these isolates also act as common isolates. The application of these three types of isolates in CC is briefly presented to you in the succeeding sections of this unit.

2.2 TIME ISOLATE

Chapter 3, part (P 1.49) of CC deals with the theoretical aspects of Time isolate with few worked out examples. Chapter 3, Part 2 (2.7) of CC provides chronological divisions (T1) and featured time isolates (T2). In the (MC) V History (T) is very essential facet. Many of the common isolates are fitted with (T) or with (P) got by chronologic device (CD). When a specific title warrants we can use T1 and T2 separated by the connecting symbol single inverted comma. T1 is represented by Indo-Arabic numerals and T2 represented by the combination of Roman small letters and Indo-Arabic numerals.

2.2.1 Chronological Divisions (T1)

The first digits A and its divisions represents Various geological ages from Ezoic to Quaternary (A1 to A5). The digit B to YC represent 9999 BC to 3199 AD. We can represent any particular year, decade or century. The distribution of digits to represent different time spans is not even.

A represent before 9999 BC

A1 to A5 represent geological ages

B represent second to tenth millennium BC i.e. 9999 to 1000 BC

C represent first millennium BC i.e., 999 to 1 BC

D represent the first millennium AD1-999 i.e., first 1000 years.

E to YC represent a century

2.2.2 BC Number

To determine the digits of BC number, Ranganathan devised a method, which is called Method of Compliments. This method consists of subtracting the year to be denoted from the higher numerical limit denoted by that digit. For example we wish to represent1100 BC. This period 1100 BC is covered by the space represented by that digit B. The highest limit represented by B is 9999 BC. So to denote 1100 BC it must be subtracted from 9999. Thus 1100 BC is denoted as (9999-1100) B8899. Like wise 4000 BC is denoted by B5999, 7000 BC is denoted by B2999 and so on. Similarly 999 BC is indicated by C000, 20 BC indicated by C 979, and 2 BC represented by C 997.

D represents the first millennium AD. A century in it is be indicated by adding the digits of the century – 0, 1. Or 9 as the case may be after D. A decade is to be indicated if necessary by adding the digit of the decade 0,1 or 9 as the case may after the century digit. For example 1 AD is indicated by D001, 20 AD is indicated by D020, 551 AD is indicated by D551.

2.2.3 Effective Decade

According to Ranganathan a generation is a natural and significant unit in the progress of human affairs. A decade is arbitrary and arithmetical. Effective decade consisting two decades makes the work of classifier less difficult than a decade or a year. He postulates the digits, 1,3,5,7 and 9 is effective decade digits. The following table give us the idea of using an effective decade.

Effective decade digits	Actual decades Digits	Span of the years of the Century
1	0 or 1	0-19
3	2 or 3	20-39
5	4 or 5	40-59
7	6 or 7	60-79
9	8 or 9	80-99

Let us take for example the ED for 1982 is N9, for 1900 AD ED is NI, for 1769 ED is L7 and for 1779 ED is also L7, and for 1945 the ED is N5.

As stated already each letter or letter group E to YC represents a century. For example 1045 AD=E45, 1900-N00, 2001 AD=P001, 2005 AD=P005.

The following examples give us the idea of use of time isolates.

History of India brought upto 1947	V44 'N47
Public Library development in India during the 20th century	22.44 'N
Industrial development in India during 1970's	X.8 (A):89ZB.44'N 7

2.2.4 Featured Time Isolates (T2)

The featured time isolates is given in part 2, P2.7.There is no much explanation about time schedule in part 1. The isolates represent seasonal meteorological and other aspect of a day. A single inverted comma is to be inserted between T1 and T2 (See rule 392, P 1.50) The following worked out examples demonstrate the use of (T1) and (T2).

1.	Winter sports in India	MY.44 'N7
2.	Night Temperature	U284 'd
3.	Dry weather conditions in A. P. in 1999	U281.4416 'N99
4.	Harvesting of wheat during spring season in Punjab in 1998	J381:7.4443 'N98
5.	Refuse disposal in England during snow period	D886.561 'p1

2.2.5 Geological Ages

As told to you already the alphabet A and its divisions A1 to A5 stand for geological ages or periods. In the case of books dealing with Paleontology, Paleontology and Plaeozoology, time isolates are not be taken from Chap 3. Part 2 P. 2.7, but from subdivisions given in H5 stratigraphy. The alphabet A should replace H5 (See rule H68 u P1.80)

The following are few worked out examples.

1. Cambrian Paeleozoology H6' A21
2. Jurassic Palaeobotany 1:8 'A33
3. Cainozoic stratigraphy of India H5.44' A4
4. Fish fossils of Triassic period H692' A31

NOTE: As per rule H6 part 2, P.1.80, H6 should be sharpened by the Natural Group Number of Zoology. Analysis of class no. H6 92' A31 H6 Palaeontology (MC) 92 pices (fish) taken from (P) of Zoology. A31 Triassic period. Taken from H531 stratigraphy as per the rule at page 1.80 H5 is to be replaced by A.

Self Check Exercise 1

Assign the class number for the following titles using T1 and T2 and H5 stratigraphy wherever required

(a) Rainfall during winter 1998.
(b) Harvesting of wheat during summer 1997.
(c) Winter games in Alps mountains.
(d) Occurrence of Asthama during wet period.
(e) Storing of horse feeding during autumn.
(f) Observation of atmospheric pressure during day times in 1997
(g) Expedition to Mount Everest during summer 1998.
(h) Animal fossils of Cambrian period.
(i) Quaternary paleobotanical surveys in India.
(j) Bird fossils of Jurassic period.

2.3 SPACE ISOLATE

Chapter 4 part 1, P1.51 deals with theoretical aspects of space isolate with few worked out examples. Chapter 4 part2, P2.8 to 2.17 provides for the geographical divisions (S1) and physical divisions (S2). In annexure at page 26 revised schedule for physical features is provide. You have to use this schedule whenever you are require to represent physical features in the class number. Isolates in (S1) aré denoted by Indo-Arabic numerals and those of (S2) isolates are denoted by Roman Small alphabets. The schedule of space isolates admits of four Blocks viz. 1. Physiographical features, 2. Political divisions 3. Population Clusters and orientation divisions.

As stated already it is common fact that many subjects are qualified by space. The connecting symbol for space facet is do (.).As per rule 492 part 1, P1 .53 a dot is to be inserted as the connecting symbol between (S) and S2).

The digit 1 is used represent world as a integral unifocal sense. It is further divided by 1-0 Empire, 19 by Zone, 19 A Orientation, 2 Mother Country, 3. Favoured country and 4-8 represent continents and countries. The digit 9 represents isolands and oceans. Many more aspects of space can be constructed by Geographical, Chronological and subject devices.

2.3.1 Empires, Zones and Orientation

In CC empires are represented by super-imposition device. Take for example: Spanish Empire 1-541, Italia Empire 1-52 (See rule 41-2, Part P1.51) French India 44-53.

The various zones of the world such as Equatorial, Tropical, Sub-arctic etc are represented by dividing the digits 19.

Let us take for example:

1. Agriculture in Tropical regions of the world J.192
2. Weather conditions in sub aretic regions U28.197
3. Natural history of sub tropical regions G:12.193
4. Library architecture in temperate zone NA, 22.195

Any geographical division may be further divided by Orientation divisions of 1 world by orientation divisions given in the schedule from 19 A to 19Y(See rule 47, Part 1, P1-52). The orientation divisions to be attached to any geographical area by dropping the initial digit 1 from the orientation number.

Let us take few examples:

1. Education in North East India T.1449**W** (~~1~~**9W**)
2. Political conditions in West Asia W.49**M** (~~1~~**9M**)
3. Social condition in North-West Africa Y.69**R** (~~1~~**9R**)
4. Cooper mining in South-West AustraliaHZ113.9**L** (~~1~~**9L**)

NOTE: According to rule HZ1 (P1.82) and H1.1 (P.1.80)

Personality isolates for HZ, mining have to be taken from (P) of E Chemistry.

2.3.2 Organisations with Near Sovereign Powers:

According to rule 4.12 (P1.51) countries falling in two or more continents coming together under an organization with near sovereign powers, is to be derived from 1 by Chronological Device (CD).Here are few worked out examples:

1. History of United Nations V1N4

NOTE: UN was established during fag end of second world war. Hence decade N4 i.e. 1940's was taken as a focus.

2. Higher education in Common Wealth Countries T4.1N48

NOTE: Commonwealth was founded in 1948.

3. Defense Policy of Non-aligned Movement Countries (1955) V:19 (zp). 1 N 55

NOTE: As per rule 47 (P1.52) CD can be applied to countries comming together under one organisation in one continent or states coming to gather in one country

1. Common Currency of European Union (1998) X 61.5N98
2. Trade among Association of South East Asian Nations (1967) X:5.43 N67
3. Poverty in Organisation of American States (1948) Y:433.7N48

2.3.3. Countries falling under a Subject

According to rule 413 (P1.51) the isolate number of an area made of countries falling in two or more countries, but deemed as the unit focus on the basis of subject characteristic, is to be divided from 1 by (SD). Here are few worked out examples.

1. Book Publishing in French speaking countries M16.1 (P122)
2. Customs and traditions in Muslim countries Y:356.1 (Q7)
3. Land laws in coffee growing countries Z, 211.1 (J481)

NOTE: As per rule 47 (P1.52) (SD) can be applied to countries filling under one continent or states coming together in country on the basis of subject characteristic.

1. Secondary Education in French speaking states of Africa T2.6 (P122)
2. Economic geography of wheat growing states of India U6.44 (J382).
3. Religious practice in Buddhist countries of Asia Q:4.4 (Q4)

2.3.4 Physical features

The isolates in (S2) are physical features. Revised rules and schedule for physical feature are given in annexure at page 21 and 26.You have to be familiar with revised rules and schedule.

As per rule 4A2 (P21) a dot is to be inserted as the connecting symbol (CS) before the isolate number of a physical feature if it follows the (IN) of a political division.

As per rule 4A3 (P21) a physical feature is to be individualized by (AD). Here are few worked out examples.

1. Horticulture in the Godavari valley J1.441.glG
2. Skating in the Himalayas MY254.g7H
3. Ecology of Vindhya Mountains G:5.44.g7V
4. Navigation in Amazon river MD525.7p1A

2.3.5 Population Cluster

As per rule 4B1 (P22) the (IN) for a population cluster or locality is to be got by (AD). As per the rule 4B2 (P22) a dot (.) is to be inserted as (CS) before the (IN) of population cluster. Here are few workedout examples.

1. Computer education in Hyderabad City in 1990's T (D6, 8 (B)). 4416.H'N9
2. Streeteleaning in Srinagar during winter D885.4447 S 'N7
3. Cinema theatres in North Zone of Bangalore NW.4413.B9s

   As per rule C4 (P23) an orientation division may have to follow the population cluster.
4. Prevention of crime in south Mumbai city Y:45:5.4435.M.9G
5. Tirupathi Sthalapurana Q22:38.4416.T

Self Check Exercise 2

Assign class numbers for the following titles using (S1) and (S2) isolates

(a) Flora and fauna of temperate zones.

(b) River transport in Northwest India

(c) Gold mining in South West Natal Province

(d) Cultural relations among Organization of African Unity (OAU) countries (Estd. 1963)

(e) Prevention of cruelty to animals in Buddhist countries.

(f) Freed trade among coffee growing countries in the world

(g) Floriculture in Kaveri valley

(h) Navigation on river Nile

(i) Management Education in Mumbai city

(j) Hospital facilities in Chennai

2.4. LANGUAGE ISOLATE

Chapter 5 (P1.54) of CC present theoretical aspects of Language Isolates. The schedule is in Chapter 5 (2.26). These isolates are mainly used in Linguistics and Literature when a particular languages acts as personality isolate. These isolates are also sparingly use a in the (MC) Generalia bibliography and to represent language facet in the Ranganathan's facet formula for Book number. Some of the important families of languages have been enumerated from isolate numbers 1 to 3 (P2. 26). The schedule also provides major Indian Languages. Many prominent languages have not been listed. But the theory part (P1.54) provides rules for their representation in the class numbers. The important divisions in the language schedule is as follows (P2.26).

1	Indo-European Languages
12	Latin
13	Greek
14	Slavonic
15	Sanskrit
16	Italian
2	Semitic languages
3	Dravidian languages
4-9	Other languages (to be got by (GD))
9-9	Artificial languages (to be got by (CD))

2.4.1 Languages not listed in the Schedule

As per rule 51 (P1.54) to represents a particular language not listed in the schedule but definitely belong to one of the three families represented by digits 1,2 and 3, the digit a should be added after the number of the ultimate division into which it will fall and the digit 9 should be further extended by (GD). Here are few worked out examples.

1. Finish Linguistics P119575

   (Note:575 is Finland)
2. Georgian literature O1497323

   (Note: 7323 Georgia)
3. Turkish phonetics P29591

   (Note: 591 is Turkey)

2.4.2 Other Languages

According to rule 54 (P1.54) Asian, African, American, Australian and other languages belong to classes 4 to 9should be individualized by (GD). The geographical isolate in which it first became current should be used in the (GD). Here are few worked out examples.

1. Grammar of Chinese languages P 41:2 (41 China)
2. Syntax in Bulgarian language P5922.3 (5922 Bulgaria)
3. Tibetan poetry O498, 1 (498 Tibet)
4. Abysianian fiction O682,3 (682 Abyssinia)
5. Bibliography of Mongolian manuscripts a 12-3496 (496 Mangolia)

2.4.3 Artificial Languages

As per rule 55 (P1.54) the (IN) for an artificial language should be got by (CD) using the year in which it was coined as the epoch. In the schedules (P2.26) CC provided illustrative examples of artificial languages under digit 99. Here are few worked out examples.

1. Teaching Esperonto T:3 (P99M87)
2. Accent in Volpauk P99M8:12

3. Sentences in Novial (1928) P99N28,6
4. Figure of speech in Interglossa (1940s) P99N4:75
5. Readers for learning Savara Language P99N4:75

Note: Savara is a Hill tribe living in mountain regions of the Northern Andhra Pradesh. The language was developed in 1930's:

2.4.4 Favoured Language

As per rule 55 (P1.54) if libraries possess extensive collection of books in Literature and Linguistics of the favoured language for example English or Telugu or Hindi than other languages, the language number of such language may be replaced by '- (Hyphen) in the class number. Here are few worked examples:

1. English Fiction O-, 3
2. Telugu Drama O-, 2
3. Hindi Poetry O-, 1
4. Genders in Kannada P-:22
5. Tamil Phonetics P-:1

Self Check Exercise 3

Assign class numbers for the following titles using language isolates.

(a) Structure of Thai language
(b) Burmese poetry
(c) Malay syntax
(d) Readers for learning café Afan
(e) Dictionary of Volapauk
(f) Korean literary criticism
(g) Romanian drama
(h) Hungarian Grammar
(i) English oration (Note: English is favoured language)
(j) Modern Telugu syntax (Note: Telugu is favoured language)

2.5 SUMMARY

In the proceedings sections you have been introduced to the treatment of Time, Space and Language Isolates. In CC Time and

Space are two of the fundamental categories. These two are common to all the main classes listed in CC. Language isolates are common to the main classes literature and linguistics.

Time isolates appear at two levels. Level 1 consists of chronological divisions and Level 2 featured time isolates. The application of these two types are amply demonstrate with worked out examples.

Language isolate is used mainly in the main classes literature and Linguistics. The schedule will provides for the devices for coining numbers for languages not listed in the schedule, other languages and artificial languages. The use of this schedule is amply demonstrate with worked out examples.

Especially Time and Space isolates contribute to the synthetic nature of C.C.

2.6 KEY WORDS

Favoured Language: Language of the majority of the books actually or intended to be included in the library.

Featured Space Isolate: Physiographical feature smaller than a continent or an ocean and man made formations and population clusters. Eg: Valley, Plateau, Desert, Mountains etc.

Featured Time Isolate: Pocket of time repeating itself in the stream of time as a result of astronomical factors.

Orientation Division: Division of the surface of the earth or of a geographical area based on orientation as a characteristic.

Population Cluster: An area with a high density of population and with certain community centres.

Zone: Division of surface of the earth or of a georapical area based on latitude as a characteristic.

2.6 ANSWERS TO SELF CHECK EXERCISES

Exercise: 1

(a) U2855 'N98'N7

(b) J382: 7: 7' N97'N3

(c) MY.5.g7A'n7

(d) L44: 453'p5

(e) KZ442:1:8'n5

(f) U282:fN97'C

(g) U8.4.g7E'N98'n3

(h) H6'A21

(i) I:844'A5t4

(j) H696'A33

Exercise:2

(a) G:12.195

(b) X423.449R

(c) HZ 118.6329L

(d) Y:1.6N63

(e) R47.1(Q4)

(f) X:533.I(J481)

(g) J16.441.glkf)

(h) MD 525.6.plN

(i) Tx:8.4435.M

(j) L:14.4411.C

Exercise-3

(a) P433:2

(b) 04 38,1,

(c) P435:3

(d) P99M86,9

(e) P99M8:4k

(f) 0495:g

(g) 01495921,2

(h) P1495932:2,

(i) 0-,5,J)P-,J:3

2.8 ASSIGNMENT

Assign class numbers to the following titles using Time,

Space and Language isolates where necessary.

1. Agricultural development in Northwest China during 1990s.
2. Summer Olympics in Sweden during 1998.
3. Cretaceous bird fossils of Java.
4. Freedom struggle in British India during 1940.
5. Climatic conditions in arctic region.
6. Population growth in Eastern African countries.
7. Economic development of SAARC (Estd. 1985)
8. Rural development in Spanish speaking countries of the world.
9. Winter games in Alps Mountains.
10. Verbs in Mangolian language
11. Words in Bantoo language.
12. Clauses in Interlingua.

2.9 SUGGESTED READINGS

1. Raju, AAN. 1984. *Decimal, Universal Decimal and Colon Classification* Ajanta Publications, Delhi.
2. Ranganathan, S.R. 1962. *Elements of Library Classification* 3rd Edition, Asia publishing House, Bombay.
3. ———————————1969. *Colon Classification* 6th Edition, Reprint. Asia Publishing House, Bombay.

UNIT 3

Common Isolates

---

0 Objectives 1 Introduction 2 Anteriousing Common Isolate (ACI) 3 Posteriorsing Common Isolate (PCI) 4 Summary 5 Key Words 6 Answers to Self check Exercises 7 Assignment 8 Suggested Readings

---

3.0 OBJECTIVES

In unit 2, we have introduced you to the application of Time, Space and Language isolates. This unit deals with the application of Anteriorising and Posteriorising common isolates (ACI and PCI).After going through this unit you will be able to:

- Understand the meaning of common isolate
- Recognise various types of common isolates provided in C.C.
- Apply (ACI) and (PCI) in the construction of class number as per rules and worked out examples.

3.1 INTRODUCTION

Chapter 2, P1.43 of CC deals with theoretical aspects of Common Isolate (C1). Each division in a facet is said to be an isolate. Common Isolate is attachable to many classes of many main classes. These are listed in chapter 2, P2.5. In other words these act as common activities in CC. Ranganathan has identified a variety of Common Isolates. The following chart gives us the idea about various types of (CI) treated in CC.

Special isolates are special to various main classes falling under (P) (M) (E) facets. A common isolate can be attached to several host classes, which is denoted, by same idea, same term and same number. The application of these are presented in the following subsections.

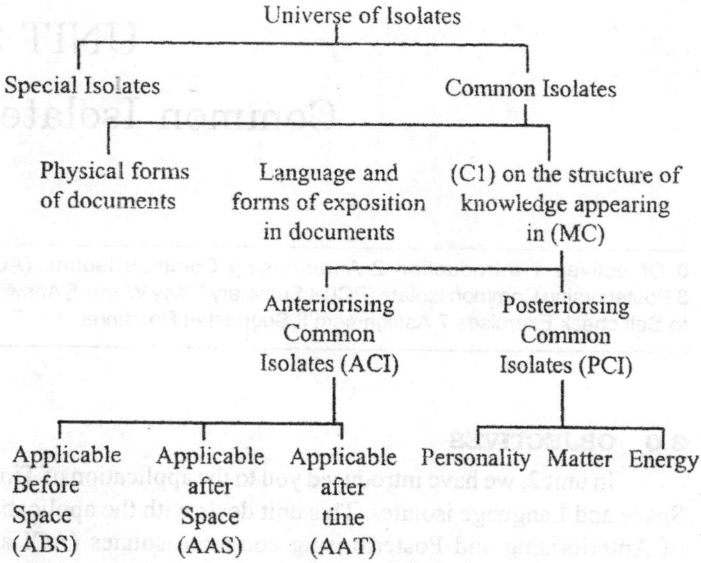

3.2 ANTERIORISING COMMON ISOLATE (ACI)

A (C1) attachable to host class number directly without a connecting symbol is an ACI. The attachment of an (ACI) to a host class makes the resulting class have the precedence in arrangement over the host class. The use of ACI is specified in rule 203. P1.43. The class number is to be worked out on the basis facet formula prescribed in chapters 9z to Z of the schedules to the fullest extent admitted by the specific subject, and later the relevant (ACI)has to be attached. When ever required two or more (ACI) may be attached in succession (Rule 2032,Pl.43).

Example: Syllabus and Synopsis of Library Science in India brought up to 1990s. 2 y2 y344'N9.

Most of the (ACI) are to be filled with one or two personality facets as prescribed in chapter2 of the schedules (P2.5). The isolates of two personality facets are to be got by (CD) and (CD) respectively. As per rule 206 (Pl.44) when both facets prescribed are required to be used, the facet by the (GD) is to be put first. And the tow facets are to be separated by comma (,). A table of facets for (ACI) is given at section 21 (P1.45) Please refers this table.

3.2.1. (ACI) Applicable before Space Facet

Chapter 2 (p 2.5) provides a schedule of CIs applicable before Space Facet. The use of some of these isolates are given below with worked out examples: For some of ACI (ABS) we find facet formula. As per the facet formula we have to attach an ACI (ABS) to a host class.

1. Shakespeare concordance 0111,2564c
2. Bibliography of Physics published in 1998.

   Ca'N98

   k Cyclopedia k[P], [P2]

   ↓ ↓

   (GD) (CD)
3. Encyclopedia Americana, N.Y. 1976

   (This is a general encyclopedia)

   k 73,N 76
4. International Encyclopedia of Social Sciences, N.Y. 1967

   Σ K73, N67

   m Periodical m[P], [P2]

   ↓ ↓

   (GD) (CD)
5. Annals of Library Science and Documentation, 1997.

   (This is Library Science Periodical published from India)

   2m44,N79

   n Serial N[P], [P2]

   ↓ ↓

   (GD) (CD)
6. Directory of Indian Scientific periodicals, 1976.

   (This was brought out by INSDOC)

   Amn44, N76

Note: As per the rule 2032 (P1, 43), we can use two (ACI).

7. Manorama Year Book, 1997. zn44, N97

   Note: This is a general reference book, therefore we use z

i.e. zeneralia main class. (See Chapter 9z P1.62)

p Conference Proceedings p [P], [P2]
↓ ↓
(GD) (CD)

8. Proceedings of Indian Science Congress held at Hyderabd 1998.

   Ap44, N98

9. Proceedings of International Geographical Conference held at Moscow in 1997.

   Up1, N97

   Note: The scope of Conference is *International*. Therefore, we have to use 1 (world) to represent [P] i.e. by Geographical Device (GD).

   w Biography

   General w [S] [T2]
   ↓ ↓
   Space Time

   Individual [P]
   ↓
   Year of birth

   Auto biography w [P], 1
   Ana (collection of one's talks etc) w[P], 2
   Letters w [P],4

10. India who's who, 1976 w44 N7)

    Note: As per rule 21 w5 (P1.47) collective biography of persons of a specific geographical area, the digit w is to be fitted with two personality facets i.e. by (GD) and (CD).

11. Dictionary of National Biography, 1971

    w56,N7

12. Biography of Srinivasa Ramanujan (1858) BwM58
13. Biography of S.R. Ranganathan (1892-1972)2wM92.

EXCEPTIONS

As per rule V9y7 (P1.116) biography of a king, president, a minister, a legislature, a leader of a political party y7 case study is to be used instead of .

14. Biography of Jawaharlal Nehru (1889-1964) V44,21y7 M89
15. Biography of a Rajendera Prasad (1884-1963) Dr. Rajendra Prasad was the first President of India. V44, 1y7M84
16. My experiments with Truth by M.K. Gandhi (1884-1948) (This is an autobiography of Mahatma Gandhi) V44:51 y7 M69,1
17. Roses in December by M.C. Chagla (1900)(This is an autobiography MC. Chagla former Chief Justice of Bombay High Court) Z44, 83, 11w N00,1
18. Speeches of J. Krishna Murthy (1895-1986) R6 w M95,2
19. Letters of C.V. Raman (1888-1970)

    x Works (Collection or Selection)

    General x[S] '[T]

    Individual x [P]

    Year of birth of the individual is to be got (CD)
20. Collected works on Geology published in India during 1980's Hx44'MN8
21. Collected works of Sri Aurobindo (1872-1950) R6 x M72

    Y7 Case study same as for w
22. Biography of Trai Linga Swamy (1607-1887)

    Note: As per rule Δ 9y7 Page 1.94 the (ACI) number for lives of mystics and realized persons is y7 and not w. Therefore the class number for the above title is

    Δ2y7K07
23. Andhra Saints by Prof B. Rama Raju Published in 1998. Δ2y7x4416 'N98

SELF CHECK EXERCISE 1

Assign class numbers to the following titles using ACI (Applicable before space facet)

1. Bibliography of Hinduism brought up to 1970
2. Rabindranath Tagore's (1861) Concordance
3. Historical Atlas of India of 19th century
4. Mc. Graw Hill Encyclopedia of Science Technology (4th Edn. 1977)
5. Library Science with slant to Documentation and Information Management for the year 1997.
6. Statesman's year book (1864) London, Mac Millan
7. Hyderabad Telephone Directory for the year 1997
8. Proceedings of International Monetary conference held at Vienna, 1996
9. 'Wings of fire', an auto biography APJ Abdul Kalam (1931)
10. Biography of Sri Ramakrishna Paramahamsa (1836-1886)

3.2.2 (ACI) Applicable only After Space Facet

1. Administration report of Dept. of Public Libraries, Govt. of A.P. for the year 1998   22.4416 r N98
2. Annual higher education statistics, govt. of India 1998 T4.44s N98

3.2.3 (ACI) Application only after time Facet

1. Kothari Commission Report,1966 (This is a report on higher education India) T4.44'N66t
2. Report of Advisory Committee for libraries, 1959 (This report deals with Public Libraries in India) 22.44'N59t
3. Ninth Five Year Plan (1997-2002) Govt. India 1998 X:75.44'N98t5
4. Source Material on India history, Published in 1998 V44'N98v
5. Stray statistics on urban accidents in India Published in 1972 Y33:437.44'N72s
6. Survey report on rural dwellings in AP Published in 1997 NA4416,31'N97t4

Self Check Exercise 2

Assign class numbers to the following titles using ACI (Applicable only after Space and Time)

1. Monthly Statistics of the foreign trade of India 1917.
2. Statistical Abstract, India (Annual, 1975).
3. Administration Report of UGC.
4. Report of Tariff Commission govt. of India for the year 1992
5. Report of Agriculture prices commission, govt. of India for the year 1995
6. Source material on India archeology published in 1965.
7. Insurance archives, 1995
8. Survey Report on Rural Destitution in India, 1996.

3.3 POSTERIORISING COMMON ISOLATE (PCI)

A (C1) needing a connecting symbol for attachment to a host class number is a (PCI). The attachment of those isolates to a host class makes the resulting class succeed the host class. For example evaluation of a work in a class succeeds the work in the class. Institution pertaining to a class succeeds the class.

In CC at Page 2.6 we find the schedule for PCI (P) and PCI (E) isolates. PCI (M) are not listed. The rules stated at Page 1.48 have been slightly modified in respect of PCI (P). The modified rules are given in annexure at page 20. While applying PCI (P),you have to follow the modified rules.

3.3.1 Energy Common Isolate

When ever you apply PCI (E) you have to fit with connecting symbol: Colon Here are few worked out examples:

1. Literary criticism 0:g
2. Critical evaluation of Telugu Poetry 035, 1:g
3. Designing library classification schemes 2:51:b2
4. Investigation in to accident in mines HZ:44:f
5. Experiments in Analytical Chemistry E:3:f3
6. Surveying underground water in Andhra Pradesh H4 224.4416:u

Self Check Exercise 3

1. Investigation of Urban Crimes
2. Observation of Lunar Eclipse
3. Designing Physics Curriculum
4. Criticism of War and Peace of Totstoy (1828-1910)
5. Drafting Library Law
6. News reporting

3.3.2 (PCI) Personality common Isolate

As per rule 27 (P1.48) a PCI should be generally added after [S]

As per rule 271 a PCI is to be fitted water [P]. The isolate in (P) is to be got be (AD) if localized body or by (CD) if it is a non localized body. As per rule in the annexure at page 20, "Add at the end, the (CD) number should be proceeded by 9'' The (P) should be preceeded by a comma'',

As per rule 272 at page (1.48) a (PCI) may be fitted when warranted with (P2) (E) and (T) as the (MC) V History.

The following facet formula for PCI (P) is given at page 2.6

(CI), (P), (P2) : (E) → Same as [P2] and [E] of V History

(P) → To be got by (AD) if localized body

(CI) ↓ Common Isolate

OR

Isolate to be got by (CD) if non-localised body

- As per modified rule 271 at page 20 (annexrue) the (CD) number should be preceeded by "9''.The [P] should be preceeded by a comma.

The following are few worked out examples.

1. Higher Educational Institutions T,e4 or T4,e
2. Physics Laboratory C,f3
3. Astronomical observations in India B9,44,f2
4. Annual Report of National Physical Laboratory (Estd.1952) for the year 1997 C.44. f3,9,N52'N97

5. Report of the Functions of the Vice-Chancellor of Osmania University for the Year 1998. T.4416, e4, OU, 12:3'N98r
6. Constitution of Indian Library Association (Estd.1930) 2.44,b9, N30:2
7. Report of the Indian Council for Cultural Relations (Est. 1950) for the year 1996 Y:1.44,g,9,N50'N96r
8. History of Bombay Natural History Society G:12.44, 9H83V

SELF CHECK EXERCISE 4

Assign class numbers to the following titles using (PCI) Personality common Isolate.

1. Mathematical society
2. Annual report of the Federation of Indian chambers of Commerce and Industry (Estd. 1960) for the year 1996.
3. Functions of Vice Chancellor of A.P. Agricultural Univrsity, Hyderabad.
4. Functions of the President of IASLIC (Estd. 1956), Calcutta.
5. Annual Report of International Federation for Information and Documentation (FID) (Estd. 1938) for the year 1998.
6. Annual report of the Director General of International Atomic Energy Agency (IAEA, Estd. 1957) for the year 1997.

3.4 SUMMARY

Common Isolates can attached to several host classes, which are denoted by the same isolate term, represented by the same isolate numbers. In CC there are two types of common Isolates. These are Anteriorising Common Isolate (ACI) and Posteriorising Common Isolate (PCI). (ACI) can be attached to any host class without any connecting symbol. Ranganathan has identified three types of (ACI). These are: 1. Applicable only before Space Facet. 2. Applicable only after Space Facet and 3. Applicable only after Time Facet. An (ACI) attached to a host class makes the resulting class have precedence in arrangement over the host class.

Posteriorising Common Isolates have to be attached to any host class with their respective connecting symbols. A (PCI) attached to a host class makes the resulting class to succeed the host class. There are three types of (PCIs) viz: Personality, Matter and Energy. But the schedule for Matter Common Isolates are not found in the 6t[h] Edn. of C.C. The worked out examples amply demonstrate the utility of (ACI) and PCI) in achieving coextensive class number.

3.5. KEY WORDS

Anteriorising Common Isolate (ACI):

Common Isolate whose attachment to a host class makes the resulting class have precedence over the host class.

Common Isolate:

Isolate that can be attached to several host classes denoted by the same isolate term and isolate number.

Posteriorising Common Isolate (PCI):

Common Isolate whose attachment to a host class makes the resulting class succeed the host class.

3.6 ANSWERS TO SELF CHECK EXERCISES

Exercise-1

1. Q2aN70
2. 0157, 1M61C
3. V44fM
4. Fk73, N77
5. 2:97m44, N97
6. n56, M64
7. X36 n4416, HYD, N97
8. X61 pl, N96
9. AwN31,1
10. Δ2y7M36

Exercise-2

1. X:5.44 sN97
2. Z44sn44,N75
3. T.44,e4,9,N5r

4. X:53.44'N92t
5. X8(J):76.44'N95t
6. V44:71'N95
7. X81'N95 298
8. Y31:43.44'N96t4

Exercise-3

1. Y33:45f
2. B92:57:f2
3. T:2(C):b2
4. 0142, 3M28,1:g
5. 2(Z):p
6. 4:r

Exercise-4

1. B,g
2. X5.44,k,9,N60'N96r
3. J.4416,e4,APAU,12:3
4. 24.44,b,9,N56,1:3
5. 2:97.1,b,9,N38'N98r
6. C9B3:11.1,f,0,N57,1'N97r

3.7 ASSIGNMENT

Classify the following titles using (ACI) and (PCI)

1. Who's who in Library Science India, 1996.
2. Journal of Indian Botanical society (the first volume was published in 1919)
3. Bibliography on Psycho analysis, 1971.
4. Directory of Plywood Industry in India for the year 1996.
5. Dictionary of engineering mechanics
6. History of Printing of India
7. Biography Abdul Kalam Azad (1888-1958)
8. Annual Report of the Director of National chemical Laboratory, Pune (Estd. 1952)

9. Report of the Meenambakkam Meteorological Observatory for the year 1995.
10. Criticism of Albert Camus (1913-1960) *The Price of Justice.*
11. Proceedings of Indian Sociology Conference held at Hyderabad, 1998.
12. Biography of Indira Gandhi (1917-1984).

3.8 SUGGESTED READINGS

1. Raju, AAN, 1984 *Decimal Universal Decimal and Colon Classification, a study in comparison.* Ajanta Publications, Delhi.
2. Ranganathan, SR. 1962 *Elements of Library Classification*, 3rd Edition. Asia Publishing House, Bombay.
3. ———————— 1969 *Colon Classification* 6th Edition Reprint. Asia Publishing House, Bombay.

UNIT 4
System and Special

4.0 OBJECTIVES

In Unit-3 we have introduced to the treatment of Common Isolates in CC. In this Unit, we will introduce you to the concepts 'System' and 'Special' found in CC in certain (MCs) and their application in the construction of class number. After going through this Unit you will be able to:

- Understand the concept of 'System' and 'Special'
- Know Amplified Facet Kind 1 and Kind 2.
- Apply the system Facet (SmF) and Special Facet (SpF) independently and jointly in the construction of the Class Number, and
- Apply the rules systematically while constructing a Class Number by using (SmF) and (SpF).

4.1 INTRODUCTION

In Unit 3 we have introduced you to the application of variety of Common Isolates found in CC. In this Unit you will be introduced to the concept of System and Special found in Colon Classification. In CC some of the main Classes (MCs) and Canonical Classes (CNCs) are amplified by a System and a Special. This is called Amplified Basic Class. If a subject is expounded according to a particular 'System of thought', it must be fitted with an Amplified Facet of Kind 1. This is called System Facet (SmF). A System means exposition of a basic subject in accordance with a specific school of thought. For example in the (MC) Medicine: Ayurveda, Siddha, Unani, Allopathy and Homeopathy are systems in medicine. These are listed at the end of the schedule of a (MC). As per rule 05412 (Pl.24), the focus in the System should be got by Chronological Device (CD) using date of origin of the System as the epoch. As per rule 05413 (pl.24) the focus in the (SmF) should be omitted, if exposition is according to the currently Favoured System –that is the system in which majority of the books are expounded. In CC Allopathy is the favoured system. Therefore, the Class Number L represents Allopathy. As per rule 05411 (pl.24) the (SmF) should precede all other facets of the subject. As per rule 05414 if a book deals with more than one system the focus in the (SmF) should be represented by the digit A.

If exposition of a subject is restricted to some limited range of any of its facets its (BC) must be fitted with an Amplifying Facet of Kind2. This is called Special Fact (SpF). This to be got by enumeration beginning with the digit 9 followed by a Roman Capital Letter. As per Rule 05421 (pl.24) the (SpF) should succeed (SmF) but precede all other facets. Since for some of the (MCs) we find Specials listed at the end of the schedule of that (MC) but before systems. For example in the (MC) L Medicine: Child Medicine. Female Medicine, Industrial Medicine, Aviation Medicine are some of the examples of Specials.

As per rule No. L91 (Pl.89) if an organ number (Personality Facet) is attached to 'Special Number' or 'System Number' it should be preceded by Comma (,). Like wise if a 'Special Number' is attached to a 'System Number' the former should be preceded by a Comma.

The concept of 'System and 'Special' has greatly strengthened synthetic nature of CC and helps to achieve coextensive class number. The entire schedule of a favoured system can be utilized for other 'Systems' and 'Specials' belonging to that (MC) or (BC). In no other Classification Scheme, we find the concept of Amplified Basic Class. The provision of 'System' and 'Special' in some of the (MCs) in CC are presented in the succeeding sections.

4.2 SYSTEM

As we told you in the preceding section, some of the (MCs) or (BCs) are fitted with Systems. For example we find Systems and Specials in the following (MCs); C Physics, L Medicine, S Psychology, T Education and X Economics. The treatment of 'System' in these (MCs) is given in the succeeding sub-sections with worked out examples. In Part-1 of CC at the end of Chapters C (P1.71), L (P1.89). S (P1.112) and T (P1.113) we find worked out examples. It is better if you are familiar with these worked out examples.

4.2.1 Physics

The (MC) is divided on the basis of Canonical Divisions. At the end of the schedule for Physics we find illustrative list of systems by (CD). Here are few examples.

CK Gravitation Theory

CM Kinetic Theory

CM6 Ether Theory

CN Relativity

CN1 Quantum Theory

CN2 Wave Mechanics

Here are few worked out examples.

1. Line Spectrum according Wave Mechanics CN2,5:34
   Analysis of the Class Number:
   CN2 = Wave Mechanics (System)
   ,5 = Radiation (€5)
   :34 = Band Spectrum (€5:34)
2. Kinetic Theory of heat absorption CH,4:27
   Analysis of the Class Number
   CM = Kinetic theory
   ,4 = Heat (€4)
   :27 absorption (€4:27)
3. Quantum theory of Matter CN1, 83 (€83)

Self-Cheek Exericise-1:

(a) Gravitational theory of matter

(b) Ether theory of gas

(c) Electromagnetic theory of Para

(d) Kerr effect according to wave mechanics

(e) Quantum theory of light

4.2.2 Medicine

At the end of schedule for L Medicine we find the following systems drawn by Chronological Device (CD).

LA Systems by (CD)

LB Ayruveda

LC Siddha

LD Unani

LL Homeopathy

LM Naturopathy

We also find some worked out examples at Page 1.89. These worked out examples will guide us to use System Facet in the Construction of Class Numbers. Here are few worked out examples.

1. Ayurvedic treatment of Paralysis LB, 76:411:6

   Note: As per rule L91 (P1.89) if an organ number is attached to a "Special Number" or "Systems Number" it should be proceeded by a Comma" Therefore in the above class number the organ number 76 (Sensory nerve) is proceeded by a, (Comma).

2. Homeopathic treatment of Asthama LL, 44:453:6
3. Treatment of Jaundice by Unani LD, 291:453:6
4. Control measures for diabetes by Naturopathy LM, 293:46:55
5. Treatment of rickets by Siddha system LC, 81:463:6

   Note: At pages 2.84 to 2.85 in the schedule for Medicine we find Illustrative example of specific diseases. The worked out class numbers can be made use of for classifying document falling under Medicine.

Self Check Exercise-2:

(a) Auyrvedic treatment of rickets

(b) Siddha Cure

(c) Unani treatment of diarrhea

(d) Prevention of measles through Homeopathy

(e) Control of obesity through Naturopathy

4.2.3 Psychology

At the end of the schedule for S Psychology (P2.104) we find the following illustrative example of Systems in psychology got by (CD).

SA	Systems by (CD)
SM	Experimental
SM9	Psycho analytic
SN	Gestalt
SN1	Behaviouristic
SN14	Individualistic
SN17	Reflexology
SN2	Eidetict, Typological
SN28	Field
SN36	'We'

Here are few worked out examples.

1. Psychoanalysis of Personality SM9:7
2. Behaviouristic Psychology of women SNI,55
3. Experiments among Criminals SM,65:796
4. Behaviouristic Psychology of Secret Society SN1,81

   Note: The digit 8 Social under (P) facet has to be individual ised as (P) of Y sociology.
5. Individualistic Psychology of Genius SN14,61

Self Check Exercise 3

(a) Psychoanalysis of dreams of adults

(b) Behaviouristic Psychology of females

(c) Experimental Psychology of emotions

(d) Individualistic Psychology of Criminals

(e) Gestalt system of studying personality

4.2.4 Education

At the end of schedule for T Education (P2.106) we find some of the following systems derived on the basis of (CD)

TA	Systems by (CD)
TJ	Commenius
TL	Rousseau's School
TL2	Kant's School
TL9	Man's School
TM	Manual training
TN1	Montessori School
TN3	Basic Wardha

Here are few worked out examples.

1. Teaching techniques in Basic Schools TN3:3
2. Student work in Montessori Schools TN1:4
3. Value of Manual Training in Secondary Schools in India TM, 2.44
4. Group work in Commenius system of education TJ:4,7
5. Student life in Kant's system of education TL 2:7

Self Check Exercise 4

(a) Mathematics curriculum for Basic Secondary Schools

(b) Play method of teaching in Montessori schools

(c) Manual training in Junior colleges

(d) Student life in Herbats Schools

(e) Importance of games in Plantoon School

4.2.5. Economics

At the end of schedule of X Economics (P2.114) we find the following 'System's got by (CD)

XA	Systems by (CD)
XB	War Economics
XM	Cooperative
XM2	Socialism
XN	Communism
XN1	Syndicalism
XN19	Technocracy

Here are few worked out examples:

1. Cooperative Banks in India XM,62.44
2. Management of Industries by Technocrats XN9, 8(A):8
3. Socialistic Pattern of Industrial relations XM2:97
4. Communistic Social Security XN:958
5. Syndicalism in Textile industries in India XNI,8(M7).44

Self Check Exercise 5

(a) Milk Producers Cooperatives in India

(b) Management life insurance by Technocrats

(c) Socialistic pattern of Industrial Management

(d) Communistic Industrial relations

(e) Syndicalistic management of production

4.3. SPECIAL

As defined in the preceeding section 'Special' is an exposition of a subject restricted to some limited range of any of its facets. In other worlds in CC Special stands for the field of specialization by restricting the area of study. In CC for some of the (MCs) we find specials listed at the end of schedule but before Systems. The (MCs) and (CNCs) which are fitted with specials are: C Physics, E Chemistry, G Biology, J Agriculture, L Medicine and X Economics. The following subsections deal with provision of specials and their use in the construction of class number.

4.3.1 Physics

In physics schedule at page 2.39 we find the following specials.

C9A	Specials
C98B1	Molecular ray
C9B2	Atom
C9B3	Nucleus
C9B4	B ray
C9D1	Low temperature
C9F8	High Potential

Here are few worked out examples:

1. Nuclear fission C9B3:12
2. Reflection of Molecular ray C9B1:22
3. Atom waste product C9B2:774
4. High potential Gamma ray C9F8,4
5. High temperature x-ray C9D8,3

4.3.2 Biology

At the end of schedules for G Biology (P2.52) we find the following specials:

G9A	Specials
G9B	Embryo
G9C	Child
G9D	Adolescent
G9E	Old age

Here are few worked out examples

1. Metabolism of Embryo G9B:33
2. Child Physiology G9C:3
3. Fatigue in Old age G9E:394

4.3.3 Agriculture

At the end of schedule for J Agriculture (P2 66) we find the following specials.

J9A Specials

J9D Dry Farming

J9S Soilless farming

Here are few worked out examples

1. Dry farming of Millet. J9D,387
2. Phosphatic manure in soilless farming J9S:242
3. Dry land agriculture in India J9D.44

4.3.4 Medicine

At the end of the schedule for L Medicine but before systems (P2.86) we find the following specials:

L9A Specials

L9B Embryo

L9C Child

L9D Adolescent

L9E Old age

L9F Female

L9H Tropical

L9T Aviation

L9V War

L9X Industrial

Here are few worked out examples

1. Introduction to pediatrics L9C:4:6
2. Geriatrics L9E:4:6
3. Obstetrics L9F:3
4. Tropical diseases in India L9H:4.44
5. Clothing for Industrial workers L9X:577
6. Diet regulation for air pilots L9T:4:8

4.3.5 Economics

At the end of schedule for X Economics but before systems (P2.114) we find the following specials:

X9A	Specials
X9B	Small Scale
X9D	Large Scale
X9S	Private Enterprise
X9V	Public Utility
X9W	Public Enterprise

Here are few worked out examples

1. Wags in Small Scale Industry X9B,8(A):93
2. Large Scale Paper Industry X9D,8(M13)
3. Private Commercial banks in India X9S,625.44
4. Provident fund facility in Public Utility Services X9V:9582
5. Trade unionism in Public Enterprise X9W:97D.44

Self Check Exercise-6

(a) Nuclear fusion

(b) Molecular band spectrum

(c) Child Morphology

(d) Adolescent Pathology

(e) Dry farming of oat

(f) Physiology of soilless farming

(g) Control of children's diseases

(h) Diagnosis of pregnancy

(i) Cost of production in Small Scale Industry

(j) Industrial relations in Large Scale Industry

4.4 COMBINED APPLICATION OF SYSTEM AND SPECIAL FACETS

If a particular specific subject or particular title of a document warrants the application both System and Special, we can use both in the construction of a class number. As per rule L91 (P1;89) if a 'Specials Number' is attached to 'System Number' the former should be proceeded by, (Comma). Like wise if personality isolate is attached to 'Special Number' or 'System Number' it should be preceded by comma. As per rule 05421 (Pl.24) (SPF) should succeed the (SMF) but precede all other facets. Here are few worked out examples.

1. Treatment of Skin diseases of children by Homeopathy LL,9C,87:4:6
2. Ayurvedic treatment constipation of old people LB,9E,24:451:6
3. Provident fund scheme in large scale cooperative textile industry XM,9D,8(M7):9582
4. Management of Public Enterprise by Technocrats in India XN19,9W:8.44
5. Breeding Cinchona in dry forest lands, JB,9D,641:6
6. Quantum theory of atom CN1,9B2

Self Check Exercise-7

(a) Medical benefit in cooperative small scale industry

(b) Work study in socialistic large scale steel industry

(c) Control measures of Children diseases by Homeopathy

(d) Ayurvedic treatment of female diseases

(e) Dry farming of bamboo in the forests

(f) Quantum theory of Nucleus

4.5 SUMMARY

In CC some of the (MCs) and (CNCs) are amplified by System and Special. These are called Amplified Basic class or Canonical class. If a subject is expounded according to a particular 'System of thought' it must be fitted with an Amplified Facet kind 1. This is called System Facet (SMF). A system means exposition of a basic subject in accordance with specific school of thought. Systems are got by epoch of their origin i.e. by (CD). If exposition of a subject is restricted to some limited range of any of its facets its Basic Class (BC) or Main Class (MC) or Canonical Class (CNC) must be fitted with amplifying Facet. This is called Special Facet (SPF). Specials are got by enumeration beginning with digit 9 followed by Roman capital letter.

As per rules stated in theory part of CC, if a personality facet is attached to a 'System Number' or Special Number' it should be preceeded by a , (Comma). Like wise if a 'Special Number' is attached to a 'System Number' it should be proceeded by a, (Comma).

The concept of 'System' and 'Special' has greatly strengthened the synthetic nature of CC and helps to achieve coextensive class number. In no other classification scheme we find the concept of Amplified Basic Class (AmBC).

4.6. KEY WORDS

Amplified Basic Class

A subject expounded according to a particular system of thought or school of thought.

Favoured System

A system in which majority of the books are expounded

Special

Exposition of a subject restricted to some limited range of its facets. A branch of study.

System

Exposition of a basic subject in accordance with specific school of thought.

4.6 ANSWERS TO SELF CHECK EXERCISES

Exercise 1

(a) CK,2,

(b) CM6, 28

(c) CM65, 73

(d) CN2,5:38M

(e) CN1,51

Exercise 2

(a) LB,81:463:6,

(b) LC:4:6,

(c) LD,24:452:6,

(d) LL:4232:5,

(e) LM,12:26:55

Exercise 3

(a) SM9,2:811

(b) SN1,55

(c) SM:52

(d) SN14,65

(e) SN:7

Exercise 4

(a) TN3, 2:2

(b) TN1:96

(c) TM,25,

(d) TL7:7

(e) TN:65

Exercise 5

(a) XM,8(KZ31:71).44,

(b) XN19,813:8

(c) XM2,8(A):8,

(d) XN:97,

(e) XN1:26

Exercise 6

(a) C9B3:12

(b) C9B1:33,

(c) G9C:2,

(d) G9D:4,

(e) J9D,383,

(f) J9S:93,

(g) L9C:4:55,

(h) L9F:313,

(i) X9B:26,

(j) X9D:97

Exercise 7

(a) XM,9B:95854,

(b) XM2,9D,8(F1823):89M,

(c) LL,9C:4:55,

(d) LB,9F:4:6,

(e) JB,9D,748,

(f) CNM1,9B3

4.7 ASSIGNMENT

Classify the following titles using System and Special.

(a) Cooperative large scale pharmaceutical industry.

(b) Examinations in Basic Secondary Schools in India

(c) Psychoanalysis of fear among girls

(d) Ayurvedic treatment of tapeworm

(e) Forest ecology

(f) Homeopathic treatment of measles in children

(g) Wages in cooperative large scale tobacco industry

(h) Biochemistry of protein

(i) Child genetics

(j) Dry farming of castor

4.10 SUGGESTED READINGS

1. Raju, AAN, 1984. *Decimal, Universal Decimal and Colon Classification, a study in Comparison*. Ajanta Publications, Delhi.

2. Ranganathan, S.R. 1960. *Colon Classification* 6th Edition, Asia Publishing House, Bombay

3. Sachdeva, MS. 1983. *Colon Classification, Theory Practice* 2nd Edition, reprint, Sterling Publishers, New Delhi.

4. Satija, MP 1984. *Manual of Practical Colon Classification*, Sterling Publishers, New Delhi.

BLOCK 2
TOWARDS COEXTENSIVE CLASS NUMBER

This Block introduces you to methods and notational techniques employed in CC to achieve coextensive class number. Coextensiveness means expression in a class number of the measure of incidence of each of the relevant characteristics of the subject embodied in the document concerned. The main thrust of CC is to achieve coextensive class number for both macro and micro documents. This block consists of the following three units (5-7)

Unit 5: deals with phase, intra facet and intra array relations. The various types of relations viz. General, Bias, Comparison, Difference and Influencing coming under three levels i.e. Phase, Intra facet and Intra-array is presented with suitable worked out examples.

Unit 6: deals with different devices employed in CC to achieve coextensive class number. These devices include: Chronological Device (CD); Geographical Device (GD); Subject Device (SD); Mnemonic Device (MD); Alphabetical Device (AD); Super Imposition Device (SID); Classic Device (CLD) and Favoured Category Device (FCD). The application of these devices in CC is fully demonstrated with suitable worked out examples.

Unit 7: deals with differential facets, parallel schedules and telescoped facets. The meaning of the three concepts has been explained and their occurrence in the schedules of CC is clearly demonstrated with suitable worked out examples.

UNIT 5

Phase, Intra Facet and Intra Array Relations

5.0 OBJECTIVES

In unit 4 you have been introduced to the concept of System and Special as obtained in CC. In this unit you will be introduced to the concept of phase, Intra-facet and Intra-Array Relations. After going through this unit you will be able to:

- Understand the concept of phase, Intra-Facet and Intra-Array Relations
- Know the five types of relations viz. General, Bias, Comparison, Difference and Influencing.
- Understand the subtle difference between Intra-Facet and Intra-Array Relations.
- Construct the class number for two-phased subject at three levels i.e. Phase, Intra-Facet and Intra-array
- Grasp the advantages of the three types of relations.

5.1 INTRODUCTION

The universe of knowledge is turbulent, dynamic continuous, multi dimensional and multi faceted. Due to R &D activities in all fields of human endeavor and especially in science and technology, knowledge is fast expanding giving rise to new disciplines and branches of study. Adding to this phenomena, the inter-disciplinary approach to knowledge, gave rise to the emergence of compound and complex subject fields. The application of methodology, principles, techniques of one discipline to another discipline giving raise to the emergence of two phased subjects at different stages and levels.

A scheme for library classification should be in a position to provide notational techniques for classifying such type of two-phased subjects. Colon Classification is one of such schemes, which provides notational techniques to classify two-phase subjects. Ranganathan recognize the phenomena of emerging two phased subjects at different levels and provided notational techniques. The theory part of CC at chapter 6 (P1.55) presents the concept of Phase and Intra-Facet Relations.

According to Ranganathan a subject in one-phased if it consists of only single (MC) or any of its sub classes i.e. if it is a (BC) or a (CDC).

Example

History (MC)

History of India (CDs)

A subject is Two-phased if it brings into relation two (BC) or two (CdC) or a (BC) and a (CdC).

Examples

Sociology and Psychology (Two BCs)

(First Phase) (Second Phase)

Social Pathology and Abnormal Psychology (Two CdC)

(First Phase) (Second Phase)

Psychology and Drug habit (BC and CdC)

(First Phase) (Second Phase)

The class formed by a two-phased subjects is called a complex class (CdC). As per rule 6203 (P1.55) the class number of Two-Phased specific subject is got by inserting between the class numbers of First and Second phases the connecting symbol O and an appropriate digit to represent the phase relation. Chapter

6 of the schedules (P2.28) provides schedule of phase relation.

5.2 LEVELS OF PHASE RELATION

Ranganathan has identified three levels of Phase relation in Inter Class-phase, Intra-facet phase relation and Intra-Array phase relation. Inter class phase relation means relation between the component classes of a complex class. This generally appears between two distinct (BCs) or (MCs) or Compound or Complex Classes derived from two distinct (BCs) or CMCs)

Intra-Facet phase relation means relation between the component isolates of a complex isolate. Generally this relation emerges out of combination of two isolates from same facet of the same (BC) or (MC). The facet may be [P] or [M] or {E] or [S] or [T]. Intra-Array phase relation means relation between the component array isolates of a complex array isolate. Generally this relation emerges out of combination of two isolates from two different groups of array isolates of the same facet of the same (BC) or (MC). The facet may be [P] or [M] or [E] or [S] or [T]

5.3 TYPES OF RELATIONS

Ranganathan has recognized five types of relations viz. General, Bias, Comparison, Difference and Influence. These five types of relations may occur at Phase, Intra-Facet and Intra-Array levels. Chapter 6 of the schedules (P2.28) provides schedule of phase relation.

The succeeding subsections deal with worked out examples of these five types of relations at phase, intra facet and intra array levels.

5.4 PHASE RELATION

As stated already phase relation generally occurs between two distinct (BCs) or (MCs) or two (CdC) or a (BC) and (CdC).

5.4.1 General Relation (a)

It means more or less all-comprehensive relation other than the remaining four relations. Here are few worked out examples.

1. Relation between Linguistics and Literature POaO

2. Relation between Mathematics and Physics BOaC
3. Relation between Mechanics and Light B7OaC51
4. Relation between Mathematics and Light BOaC51
5. Relation between Library Science and Journalism 2Oa4

5.4.2 Bias Relation (b)

This relation indicates that exposition of the first phase biased towards second phase that is the exposition is attached keeping in view the requirements of the specialists forming the second phase. Here are few worked out examples.

1. Mathematics of Engineers BObD
2. Statistics for Libraries B28Ob2
3. Psychology for teachers SObT
4. Ethics for Politicians R4ObW
5. Yoga for administrators R635ObV:8

5.4.3 Comparison Relation (c)

In this relation phase 1 is compared with phase 2. Here are few worked out examples:

1. Comparative study of Economics and Political Science X0cW
2. Comparative study of Botany and Agriculture I0cJ
3. Comparative study of Psychology and Education S0cT
4. Comparative study of Ethics and Aesthetics R40cR5
5. Comparative study of Religion and Philosophy Q0cR

5.4.4. Difference Relation (d)

In this relation the difference between Phase 1 and Phase 2 is expounded. Here are few worked out examples.

1. Difference between Knowledge Classification and Library Classification R2Od2:51
2. Difference between Chemistry and Technology EOdF
3. Difference between plant life and Animal life IOdK

4. Difference between Algebra and Arithmetic B1OdB2
5. Difference between Useful Arts and Fine Arts MOdN

5.4.5 Influencing Relation (g)

In these relations the influence of one subject on another subject is expounded. In such cases the influenced phase should be treated a phase 1 and influencing phase as phase 2. Here are few worked out examples.

1. Influence of Weather on Agriculture JOgU281
2. Influence of Politics on Education TOg W
3. Influence of Television on rural society Y31Og D65, 45
4. Influence of Philosophy on human personality S:70gR
5. Influence of Religion on Music NROgQ

Self Check Exercise

(a) Relation between Political Science and History
(b) Relation between Religion and Culture
(c) Law for Doctors
(d) Statistics for Teachers
(e) Comparative study of Bibliography and Library Classification.
(f) Comparative study of Chemistry and Technology
(g) Difference between wave functions and wave mechanics
(h) Difference between Biology and Biochemistry
(i) Influence Geography on Politics
(j) Influence of music on human personality.

5.5 INTRA-FACET RELATION

It means expounding the relation between two isolates in one and the same fact of a class. The Facet may be [P] or [M] or [E] or [T] of any [BC] or [CNC]. Let us take the schedule of [P] isolates from the [MC] 2 Library Science. 2 [P]; [M]; [E]; [2P]

Foci in [P]

1 Trans Local

11 World
13 National
14 Region
15 State
16 Division
2 Local
21 District
22 City
3 Academical
31 Elementary School
32 Secondary School
33 College
34 University
36 Research
4 Business
42 Industry
44 News paper office
45 Commerce
48 Govt. Department
5 Subscription
6 Special Class
61 Child
63 Prisoner
64 Hospital
65 Woman
68 Blind
69 Seafarer
95 Contact
97 Private

The [P] facet of 2 Library Science (MC) consists of type of Library Isolates. If a particular type of relation requires the use of isolates from say isolates 3 (Academic Library) and its subdivision 31, 32 ......36 with isolate 4 (Business) and its sub divisions 42, 44....48 the relation is Intra-Facet Relation. Because isolate 3 and its subdivision and isolate 4 and its subdivision are from the same [P] Facet of Library Science (MC). Like wise some documents may require the use of 1 world and its subdivision with isolate 2 and its subdivision or isolate 6 and its subdivisions. Such type of relation is called Intra-Facet Relation. The following worked out examples covering types of relations will give us the nature of Intra-Facet Relation.

5.5.1 General Relation (j)

The following worked out examples give us the idea of taking two isolates from the same facet using general type of relation.

1. Trade relations between India and Russia X:5.440j58
2. Relationship between Academic and Special Libraries 23Oj34
3. Relationship between Elementary and Secondary Education T15Oj2
4. Relationship between Jainism and Buddhism J3Oj4
5. Relationship between Advaita and Dvaita Philosophies R66Oj8

5.5.2 Bias Relation (k)

The following worked out examples give us the idea of taking two isolates from the same of (MC) for representing bias relation.

1. European preference in India's Commerce X5.44Ok5
2. Hathayoga for Jain Mystics Δ220k3
3. Classification for Documentation 2:510k97
4. Edible oil for soap manufacturing F9430k9496
5. Clinical theraupeutics L:4:310k6

5.5.3 Comparison Relation (m)

The following worked out examples given us the idea of taking two isolates from the same facet for representing comparison relation.

1. Comparative study of Indian and American constitutions V44Om73:2
2. Comparative study Christianity and Islam Q6Om7
3. Comparative study of Public and Academic Libraries 22Om3
4. Comparative study of constitution of Earth and Moon 391Om2:68
5. Comparative study of Civil and Mechanical Engineering D1Om6

5.5.4 Difference Relations (n)

The following worked out examples throw some light in taking of two isolates from the same facet of a (MC) for representing difference relation.

1. Difference between Physical and Analytical Chemistry E:2On3
2. Difference between Hindu and Muslim worship Q2On7:454
3. Difference between Family and Social ethics R4O2n3
4. Difference between Monocotyledon and Dicotylednous 17On8
5. Difference between Vira Saiva and Vaisnava Philosophies R6634On72

5.5.5 Influencing Relation (r)

The following worked out examples throw some light of taking two isolates from the same facet of a (MC) for representing influence relation. As stated earlier influenced phase becomes phase 1 followed by influencing phase i.e. phase 2.

1. Influence of John Milton (1620) on John Keats (1730) 0111,1130OrK20
2. Influence of Hinduism on Buddhism Q4Or2
3. Influence of Indirect tax on Industry X8(A) Or 729
4. Influence of Democracy on Monarchy W4Or6
5. Influence of Political parties on Local bodies in India V44, 6 Or 4

Self Check Exercise 2

(a) Commercial Relations between India and UK

(b) Relationship between Family Ethics and Social Ethics

(c) Jnana Yoga for Buddhistic Mystics

(d) Scriptures for religious preaching

(e) Comparative study of Democracy and Monarchy

(f) Comparative study of Jainism and Buddhism

(g) Difference between Vedanta and Advaita Philosophy

(h) Difference between Political Geography and Economic Geography

(i) Influence of William Shakespeare (1564-1616) on George Bernard Shaw (1856-1950)

(j) Influence of Judiciary on Civil Service in India

5.6. INTRA-ARRAY RELLATION

It means documents expounding the relation of two array-isolates in one and the same array. A facet either it may be [P] [M] [E] [S] or [T] may consists of several groups of isolates. To represent a particular type of relation in the class number if we take two isolates from the same array it results in Intra-Array relation. Let us take as an example [P] facet of Y sociology. (MC) Y [P]: [E} [2P]:[2E] [3P]

Social Group

1	By age and sex
11	Child
12	Youth
13	Old Person
15	Woman
16	Man
2	Family
3	By residence
31	Rural
32	Urban

35	City
38	Nation
394	Refugee
396	Mountain
4	By Occupation
41	Professor
45	Commerce
46	Leisured
48	Leader
49	Working class
491	Serf
492	Slave

The schedule for (P) of Y sociology consists several groups of array isolates. They are 1 by age and sex and its divisions, 2 and its subdivision, 3 and its subdivisions, 4 and its subdivision and so on. For classifying a specific title in sociology if we are using two isolates, say 11 child and 12 youth from the same array i.e. 11-12, it is called Intra-Array relations, Like wise if we are using two isolates say from 3-396 or 4-392, it is called Intra-Array relations, If we are taking two isolates say from 1and 2 or 2 and 3 or 3 and 4 and their subdivisions it is called Intra-Facet relation. We have to clearly understand the distinction between Intra-Facet and Intra-Array relations. Accordingly the symbols for respective relations (i.e. General, Bias, Comparison etc.) either for Intra facet or Intra array have to be selected and represented in the class number. Here are few worked out examples demonstrating the use of Intra array relations.

5.6.1 General Relation (t)

1. Relationship between Rural and Urban people — Y310t3
2. Relationship between industrial and Commercial Banks — X6220t5
3. Relationship between Party in office and party in opposition in India — V44,410t5

4. Relationship between Infant and Pre-adolescent psychology — S130t5
5. Relationship between College and University libraries — 2330t4

5.6.2 Bias Relation (u)

The following worked out examples throw light on taking two isolates form the same array of the same facet for representing Bias relations in the class number.

1. Role of Numimatics for construction of Genealogy — V:730u4
2. Religious Preachings for society for parish work — Q:510u7
3. Job evaluation for Merit rating — X:910u2
4. Trade route for industrial resources — U6410u72
5. Urban culture for rural people — Y330u1:1

5.6.3 Comparison Relation (V)

The following worked out example throw light on taking two isolates from the same array of the same facet for representing comparison relation.

1. Comparative study rural and urban sociology — Y310r3
2. Comparative study of District and City libraries — 210r2
3. Comparative study of Income tax and Profession tax — X7240r5
4. Comparative study of Absolute and Limited Monarchy — W410r6
5. Comparative study Lok Sabha and Rajya Sabha — V44,319r2

5.6.4 Difference Relation (w)

The following worked out examples give us an idea of taking two isolates from the same array of the same facet for representing difference relation in the class number.

1. Difference between Latitude and Longitude in Geodetic Astronomy — B9:230r4
2. Difference between Direct current and Alternating current — C6230r4
3. Difference between Qualitative and Quantitative analytical Chemistry — E:330r4
4. Difference between Anabolism and Catabolism — G:3310r2
5. Difference between Diamond and Ruby — H1910r21

5.6.5 Influencing Relation (y)

The following worked out examples give us an idea of taking two isolates from the same array of the same facet for repreșenting influence relation in the class number.

1. Influence of Classification on Cataloguing — 2:550y1
2. Influence of Vaisnavism on Saivism — Q230y2
3. Influence Mahayana Mysticism on Zen Mysticism — Δ4602
4. Influence of Royalty on Military class — Y540y1
5. Influence of Lok Sabha Rajya Sabha — V44,320y1

Self Check Exercise 3

(a) Relationship between Lok Sabha and Rajya Sabha

(b) Relationship between Top management and Executive

(c) Field work for PG and Research students

(d) Foreign Exchange for imports

(e) Comparative study of laws relating to movable and immovable property

(f) Comparative study of Tobacco and Opium habits

(g) Difference Between job classification and job rating

(h) Difference Between direct and representative type of democracy

(i) Influence of tariff on export and imports

(j) Influence of Svetambara on Digambara Budhism.

5.7 ADVANTAGES OF PHASE, INTRA FACET AND INTRA ARRAY RELATIONS

These relations increase the capacity of given notational system to individualise subjects and help to assign coextensive class numbers. These relations also increase the versatility of notational system. Without these relations, the number of (MCs) will have to be increased. The autonomy of the classifier is greatly enhanced. Especially the provision of Intra-Facet relation eliminates the need for repeating the entire number for the host subjects in second phase. Further economy is affected by the provision of Intra Array Relation in the construction of class numbers. The Intra-Facet and Intra-Array Relations satisfy the Law Parsimony. The worked out examples in the preceedings section have amply demonstrated this fact.

5.8 SUMMARY

The inter-disciplinary approach to knowledge gave rise to compound and complex subjects. The application of methodology, principles and techniques of one subject filed to another subject field gave rise to emergence of two phased subjects at different stages and levels. A scheme for library classification should be in a position to provide notational techniques for classifying such type of two phased subjects. Colon Classification is one of such schemes, which provides notational techniques to classify two phased subjects.

Ranganathan recognized the phenomena of emerging two-phased subjects at three levels viz. phase, intra facet and intra array. He has also recognized five types of relations viz. General, Bias, Comparison, Difference and Influencing at these three levels. Generally phase relation means, relation between component classes of a complex class. Intra-Facet phase Relation means relation between component array isolates of a complex array.

General relation means more or less comprehensive relation between two phases other than the remaining four relations. Bias relation indicates the exposition of first phase biased towards second phase. In comparison relation phase 1 is compared with phase2. Difference relation indicates difference between phase 1 and phses2. Influence relation indicates the influence of one subject on another subject. In such case the influenced subject should be treated as phase 1 and influencing subject as phase 2.

These Phase, Intra Facet and Intra Array relations accrue certain advantages. They are: 1 Increase the capacity of the notational system. 2. Help to achieve coextensive class number. 3. Increase the Versatility of the notational system, and 4, Achieving autonomy to the classifier.

5.9 KEY WORDS

Bias Relation

Phase relation indicating that exposition of Phase 1 is biased towards Phase 2.

Comparison Relation

Phase relation in which phase 1 is compared with phase 2.

Difference Relation

Phase relation in which the difference between phase 1 and phase 2 is expounded.

General Relation

Phase relation of a more or less comprehensive or nondescriptive kind between two phases.

Influencing Relation

Phase relation in which the influencing of phase 2 on phase 1 is expounded or phase 1 is expounded as influenced by phase 2.

Intra-Array Relation

Relation between the component array isolates of a complex array isolate.

Intra-Facet Relation

Relation between the component isolates of a complex class.

Phase

A component of a complex class or of a complex isolate or a complex array isolate as the case may be.

Phase Relation

Relation between the phases of a complex class or of a complex isolate or of a complex array isolate.

5.10 ANSWERS TO SELF CHECK EXERCISES

Exercise 1

(a) W0aV

(b) Q0aY:1

(c) Z0bL

(d) B38 ObT

(e) Aoc2:55

(f) E0cF

(g) B85OdCV2

(h) G0dE9G

(i) WogV

(j) S9OgNR

Exercise 2

(a) X5.44Oj56

(b) R4Oj3

(c) V23Ok4

(d) Q:2Ok51

(e) W4Om6

(f) Q3Om4

(g) R65On6

(h) U50n6,

(i) O111,2M56OnJ64

(j) V44,8On7

Exercise 3

(a) V44,31Ot2

(b) X:81Ot7

(c) T45O48:4.4

(d) X:57O446

(e) Z,33Or4

(f) Y:412Or3

(g) X:915Or6

(h) W61Or2

(i) X:54Oy3

(j) Q32Oy1

5.11 ASSIGNMENT

Assign class numbers to the following titles

1. Comparative study of District and City Libraries.
2. Influence of Kalidasa on Telugu Drama
3. Difference between Hinayana and Mahayana Buddhism
4. Relationship between Algebra and Trignometry
5. Mathematics for civil Engineers
6. DDC, UDC and CC, a study in comparison by A.A.N. Raju
7. The difference between Organ and clairionet music
8. Influence of Mahatma Gandhi (1869-1948) on India's freedom movement
9. The difference between Roman Catholics and Protestants
10. Foreign policy between India and China

5.11 SUGGESTED READINGS

1. Raju, AAN, 1984, Decimal, *Universal Decimal and Colon Classification, Study in Comparison*. Ajanta Publications, Delhi.
2. Ranganathan, S.R. 1960. *Colon Classification* 6th Edition, Asia Publishing House, Bombay.
3. Sachdeva, MS. 1983. *Colon Classification, Theory and Practice*, 2nd Edn. Reprint. Sterling Publishers, New Delhi.
4. Satija, MP 1984. *Mannual of Practical Colon Classification*, Sterling Publishers, New Delhi.

UNIT 6

Devices

---

0 Objectives 1 Introduction 2 Chronological Device (CD) 3 Geographical Device (GD) 4 Subject Device (SD) 5 Mnemonic Device (MD) 6 Alphabetical Device (AD) 7 Superimposition Device (SID) 8 Classic Device (CLD) 9 Favoured Category Device (FCD) 10 Summary 11 Key Words 12 Answers to Self Check Exercises 13 Assignment 14 Suggested Readings

---

6.0 OBJECTIVES

In unit 5 we have introduced you to the concept of phase, intra facet and intra array relations. In this unit you will be introduced to different devices employed in CC to sharpen the focus of any facet. After going through this unit you will be able to:

- Understand the need for provision of devices in CC
- Know the different devices employed in CC
- Find out how autonomy to the classifier is ensured
- Locate the provision of the devices in the schedules of CC; and
- Employ the devices to sharpen the focus of any facet for assigning coextensive class numbers to specific subject fields.

6.1 INTRODUCTION

As we told you already that universe of knowledge is dynamic, ever growing, multi dimensional and multifaceted. As a result, new subjects, disciplines come into existence, which call for the formation of new isolates or the sharpening of existing ones to enable the classifier to assign the coextensive number. The classifier cannot wait for revised or new edition of a scheme for classification which may take, some times, few years and therefore there should be provision in the schedules certain devices with which the classifier can assign appropriate class number for newly emerging subject fields. This is what Ranganathan called autonomy to the classifier, which is the bedrock of Colon Classification.

In Colon Classification at chapter 058 (P1.28) we find the following devices, which may be employed to form or shapen the focus of any facet

1. Chronological Device (CD)
2. Geographical Device (GD)
3. Subject Device (SD)
4. Mnemonic Device (MD)
5. Alphabetical Device (AD)
6. Super Imposition Device (SID)

In addition to the above six devices, Classic Device (CLD) and Favored Category Device (FCD) is also employed to sharpen the focus. The (CLD) is employed for bringing together different editions of a classic in a class. This device is dealt in chapter 7 (P1.59). The employment of these devices have been specified in the schedules of CC some times with illustrative examples. You have to be familiar with the use of these devices.

The following subsections deal with the application of these devices to former or sharpen the focus in any facet. The worked out examples given under each device will clearly demonstrate the utility of these devices to assign coextensive class numbers and ensure autonomy to classifier. These devices also satisfy the canons for Hospitality in Array and Chain, Consistent sequence, Helpful sequence and Mnemonics.

6.2 CHRONOLOGICAL DEVICE (CD)

CD means a device of using chronological number as an isolate number or adding to a host isolate number a chronological number. Chapter 0581 (P1.29) deals with explanation of CD. As per rule 05812 chronological numbers should be worked out to the first, or the first two or the first three digits of the year forming the epoch as specified in the rules.

The schedules of CC contain many examples in which the device is usefully employed. For example individualization of special forms and functions in 'Mathematics', fixing author numbers in 'Literature', classification of artificial languages in 'Linguistics', classification of religious sects in 'Religion' different systems in Physics, Medicine, Psychology, Education and Economics, CD ahs been applied. Here are few worked out examples employing CD.

1. Universal Decimal Classification (1896) 2:51M96
2. Rabindra Nath Tagore (1896) Gitanjali 0157,1M61,1
3. Unfinished Journey, an autobiography of Yehudi Menuhin NRw N16,1 (1916-1999)
4. IASLIC Bulletin, 1998 2m44,N98
5. 44th All India Library Conference on Libraries and Information services in Electronic Information Era, Hyderabad 25-28 February, 1999 2:977744,N99
6. Religious practice of Brahmo Samaj Q29M2:4
7. Models of Mogul Architecture (This style emerged during the 16th century i.e. 1500-1599) NA 44,J:8
8. Merrill Parma test in secondary schools (this test was formulated in 1931) T1:5,1N31
9. The grammar of Esperanto (the artificial language was formulated in 1887) P99M87:2
10. Treatment of diabetes by Naturopathy (this system was emerged during 19th century) LM, 293:46:6

Self Check Exercise –1

(a) Library Trends, Summer 1998

(b) Dewey Decimal Classification (1876)

(c) Mark Twain (1835-1910) Tom Sawyer

(d) M.K. Gandhi (1869-1948) The story of my experiments with truth

(e) XVIII National Seminar of IASLIC, Thrissur 21-24 December, 1998

(f) Preachings of Arya Samaj

(g) Preservation of Gothic Sculpture

(h) Brain test in Elementary Schools

(i) Psycho Analysis of fear of criminals

(j) Raman Effect

6.3 GEOGRAPHICAL DEVICE (GD)

(GD) consists of using geographical number or adding to a host number a geographical number that is country, state, district etc. The cases where this device may be applied are generally indicated either in the schedules or in the rules of CC. This device is applied to those languages, which do not belong to Indo-European, Semitic or Dravidian. As per rules (P1.105) (GD) is used for individualizing of dialects and jargons. The (GD) is also employed to individualize certain religions, certain communities in History and Law and at many other places in the schedules.

Here are few worked examples:

1. Indian Foreign Policy V44:19
[Here 44 India is got by (GD)]

2. French Criminal Law Z53,5
[Here 53 French is got by (GD)]

3. American Philosophy R873
[Here 73 USA is got by (GD)]

4. Anglo-Indian Jargon P111,J44,L
[Here 44 India is got by (GD)]

5. Oil colour Italian painting NQ52:4
[Here 52 Italy is got by (GD)]

6. Preservation of Greek Sculpture NA51:98
[Here 51 Greece is got by (GD)]

7. Indian Journal of Mathematics.1997. Bm44,N97
[Here 44 India is got by (GD)]

8. Features of Australian society Y78:2
[Here 8 Australia is got by (GD)]

9. Indian National Bibliography 1972 a14;144'N7
[Here 44 India is got by (GD)]

10.Indian Philosophical Congress held a Mysore, 1982
[Here 44 India is got by (GD)]

Self check Exercise-2

(a) India's Non-alignment policy
(b) British Law of contract
(c) German philosophy
(d) Rayalaseema Telugu Dialect
(e) Pallavan Orchestral music
(f) Mogul town planning
(g) Indian Journal of Biochemistry, 1999
(h) Crime in American urban society
(i) British National Bibliography, 1997
(j) First Internatinal ISKO conference on tools for knowledge organization and human inteface, Darmstadt 14-17 Augsut 1990

6.4 SUBJECT DEVICE (SD)

(SD) consists of using class number as an isolate number or adding to a host isolate number a class number. The cases where this device may be applied are indicated in the schedules or in the rules. As per rule 05832 (P1.31) subject device number should be enclosed within circular brackets. As per rule 05833 (P1.31) (SD) may be used, whenever warranted to extend the schedule in any [E]

Here are few worked out examples:

1. Documentation service in Medical Libraries 24(L):97

[Here the subject L medicine is got by (SD)]

2. Designs of paper making machinery D6,8(M13):4

[Here the subject M13 paper making is got by (SD)]

3. Models of Indian University Buildings NA44,9(T4)

[Here the subject university T4 is got by (SD)]

4. Jain Iconography ND44,E9(Q3)

[Here the subject Jain Q3 is got by (SD)]

5. Education of Middle class T9(Y53)

[Here the subject middle class Y53 is got by (SD)]

6. Adudiovisual method of teaching physics T:3(C),1

[Here the subject physics C is got by (SD)]

7. Right to property in India V44,58 (Z,2)

[Here the subject property Z,2 is got by (SD)]

8. Social security in Drug industry in India X8(F56):958.44

[Here the subject Drug F56 is got by (SD)]

As per rule 05833 (P1.31) (SD) may be used whenever warranted to extend the schedule in any [E]. Here are few examples:

9. Geophysics H:(C)
10. Medical Juris Prudence L:(4)
11. Library legislation 2: (Z)
12. Mathematical Geochemistry H: (E): (B)

Self Check Exercise-3

(a) Reference service in Technical Libraries
(b) Specifications for Brick laying machinery
(c) Architecture of British Scientific Laboratories
(d) Hindu Iconography
(e) Jain ethics
(f) Library Science curriculum in the universities
(g) Right to public health in India

(h) Medical benefits in steel industry

(i) Geomorphology

(j) Prevention of Alcoholism through News Papers

6.5 MNEMONIC DEVICE (MD)

Mnemonics means the digit used to represent a specified concept in a class number or isolate number should be the same in all class numbrs or isolate numbers having that concept represented in them. There are four types of mnemonics viz. 1. Verbal, 2. Schedule, 3. Systematic and 4. Seminal. In CC section 0584 Mnemonic Device (MD) (P1.32) deals with the applicationof Seminal Mnemonics which means using the same digit to represent seminally equivalent concepts in whatever array of whatever facet of whatever class they may appear, though the concept may be denoted by different terms in different contexts or array. Briefly it means same concept, different term, and same digit. Section 0564 (P1.32) provides a list of different possible significances of digits 1-8 available for use. According to Ranganathan this is a very powerful device, which secures high degree of autonomy to the classifier.

Here are few worked out examples:

1. Public Library Finance 22:8:7

   (Here 22:8 means public library adminstration, ther is no [2 E] Facet, but 7 can be used for finance and put under [2E]

2. Evolution of Domestic Science M3:6

   (Here digit 6 is evolution, which is seminal mnemonic)

3. Critical appreisal of aesthetics in Fine Arts N:5:g

   (Here the digit 5 aesthetics is seminal menemonic)

4. Synthesis of Oil Colours in painting NQ:4:4

   (Here the digits 4 in [2E] is synthesis, which is a seminal mnemonic)

5. Genesis of Karnatic Music NR441:6

   (Here the digits 6 under [E] is synthesis which is a seminal mnemonic)

6. Analysis of religion in Telugu Poetry 035, 1:g (Q):3

   (Here the last digit 3 is analysis, which is a seminal mnemonic)

7. the structure of Colon Classification 2:51N3:2

   (Here the digit 2 under [2E] is structure, which is a seminal mnemonic)

8. Scientific expeditions to Antarctica A:8.983

   (Here the digit 8 under [E] is travel, which is a seminal mnemonic)

Note: This title also can be classified under U8

9. Ganga Hybrid Jowar J387G:6:4

   (Here the digit 4 under [2E] is hybrid, which is a seminal mnemonic)

10. An investigation into the failures of intermediate examinations T25:5,5:4:f

    (Here the digit 4 under [2E] is failure, which is a seminal mnemonic)

Self Check Exercise-4

(a) Public library finance in Andhra Pradesh

(b) Evaluation of aesthetics in Telugu Literature

(c) Evolution of Indian Fine Arts

(d) Analysis of functions of the President of India

(e) Synthesis of religious practices

(f) Structure universe of knowledge

(g) Unity of Indian culture

(h) Hybrid rice

(i) Fitness in Athletics

(j) Value of reading lists

6.6 ALPHABETICAL DEVICE (AD)

(AD) consists of using the first or the first two or the first three etc initials letters of the international name of an isolate term or adding similarly to a host number. This device is to be used only in cases where no other method of sub-division gives a more helpful sequence. The schedules and rules indicate the places where this device has to be used. As per rule 05851 (P1.33), (AD) can be applied only in respect of proper names, trade names and certain technical nomenclature, which are internationally current. The device is employed to individualize different cultivar isolates in Agriculture, different brands of cycles and automobiles in Engineering, Authors and Individual works in literature, different corporate bodies in (PCI) personality isolate and physio-graphical feature in [S2]. Here are few worked out examples

1. J381 Rice (Varieties of rice by (AD)

   J381 B (Bangaru Tigalu)

   J381 H (Hamsa)

   J 381 M (Masuri)

   J 381 MK (Mola Kolakulu)

   J 381 SM (Sona Massuri)

   And so on
2. D 5133 Motor car (Different brands of motor cars by (AD)

   D5133 I Indica

   D 5133 M Maruti

   D 5133 MAT Matiz

   D 5133 S Santro

   D 5133 U Uno

   D 5133 Z Zen

   And so on
3. O 111, 2J64 Shakespeare, Individual works of shakes pear by (AD)

O 111, 2J64, A	As you like it
O 111, 2J64, J	Julius Ceaser
O 111, 2 J64, K	King Lear
O 111, 2J64, M	Merchant of Venice
O 111, 2J64, O	Othello
O 111, 2J64, T	Tempest
	And so on

4. I B M Computers D6, 8(B) I
5. G E C Voltameter D66e34 G
6. H M T printing machines D6, 8(M14) H
7. Osmania university, Hyderabd T.4416, e4, OU
8. Bombay Natural history Society G:12.44, g, BNHS
9. Horticulture in Godavari Valley J1.441.g1G
10. Computer Education in Hyderabad city T (D6,8(B)).4416 H
11. Catalogue of Vikas publishing House a 14,3V
12. Collected paintings of Leonardo Da Vinci NQ52xDA

Self Check Exercise-5

(a) Jersey Cow Milk
(b) V. Narayana Menon (1878-1958): Sahitya Majari
(c) Bansi Wheat
(d) Hero Honda Motor Cycle
(e) BPL Cooking Ware
(f) Andhra University, Visakhapatnam
(g) Ornithological society of India
(h) Agriculture in Kaveri Valley

6.7 SUPER IMPOSITION DEVICE (SID)

SID is used for sharpening a focus in the form of an isolate by restricting its extension to the portion of its falling within another isolate of the same facet. The connecting digit for (SID) is a hyphen (-). As per rule 05863 (P1.33) the constituent isolate that occurs earlier in the schedule normally forms the first number. This device is very sparingly employed in CC. Indiscriminate use may lead to assigning absurd class numbers. In theory part of CC we find as an example this device is employed in representing empires (P1.51).

1-52 Roman Empire
1-53 French Empire
1-56 British Empire

Again under chapter L Medicine (P1.88) we find the use of this device.

L15-82	Bones of thorax
L163-37	Arteries of the arm
L181-875	Pigment of the face

Here are few worked out examples.

1. British rule in India V44-56 (But not V56-44, which means India's rule in Great Britain)
2. Veins of arms L36-163 or L163-36
3. Telugu printed books a14-335
4. Rural Women Y15-31
5. Male Research Students T48-51
6. Psychology of middle aged females S35-55
7. Motion study of top management X:81-89 M1
8. National Agriculture Library of India 213-4(J).44
9. Architecture of Urban Hotels NA,33-44
10. Cotton-Wool blended Carpets M75, 1-2

Self Check Exercise-6

1. History of French rule India
2. Veins of Upper extremity
3. Sanskrit manuscripts
4. Personality of rural youth
5. Book Selection in College and University Libraries
6. Hostel life of PG and research students
7. Constitution of urban and rural bodies in India
8. American town and city planning
9. Sorting cotton-silk yarn
10. Telugu-Kannada Phonetics

6.8 CLASSIC DEVICE (CLD)

Classic means a work of out standing value and appearing in several versions and, or having several adaptations and translations, inspiring other works on itself and repeatedly coming in print even long after its origin. We find the classics in ever subject field and not confining only to literature. For example Kalidasa's 'Shakuntalam', Tolstoy's War and Peace, Albert Einstein's 'Theory of Relativity', Karl Marx's 'Das Capital', Ranganathan's 'Prolegomena to Library Classification', Gurajada Appa Rao's 'Kanyasulkam' (Telugu Drama), S. Radha Krishana's 'An Idealist view of Life', Jawaharlal Nehru's 'Discovery of India' and Stephen Hawking's 'A brief history of time' and so on.

Part 3 of CC deals with schedule of classics and sacred books. The class numbers for classics is constructed by employing Classic Device (CLD). Ranganathan has identified three in herent qualities of a classic (P1.59). This device is employed for bringing together different editions of a classic in a class, including commentaries and sub commentaries on different editions. As per rule 73 (P1.59) this device consists in putting the digit after the number representing the ultimate class to which the classic should be other wise assigned and adding after it an Author Facet and also a work facet. As per rule 713 (P1.60). Author and work Facets are [P]. But a comma "," need not be put between x and Author Number. The facet formula for employing (CLD) is [Class Number] x [Author], [Work], [Commentary], [Sub-Commentary]

↓

By (CD)

Here are few worked out examples:

1. LVx1,1 Charaka Samhita

   LBx1,1,1 Patanjali's commentary (First Commentary)

   LBx1,1,2 Charka Pani-Datta, Ayurveda deepika (Second Commentary)

Note: the above examples are taken from part 3 of CC (P3.3)

2. Will Durant (1885-1951) The story of civilization Y:1xM85,1

(Here the work has been treated as his first work)

3. Aurobindo Ghosh (1872-1950) Essays on Geeta R65,6xM72
4. Karl Marx: Das Capital XM2xM18,1
5. Thomas Carlyle (1765-1881) The French revolution

V53:51xL95,1

6. Charles Darwin (1809-82):On the origin of species G:66xM09,1
7. Peter F Drucker (1909): Managing for results X:8xN09,1
8. Albert Einstein (1879-1955): Theory of Relativity CNxM79,1
9. J.M. Keynes (1883-1946): Treatise on Money X61xM83,1
10. Herald J. Laski (1893-1950): Democracy in Crisis W6xM93,1

Self Check Exercise-7

(a) 'Immanuel Kant 91724-1804): A critique of Pure reason
(b) Jules Verne (1825-1905) Around the world in Eighty Days
(c) S. Radhakrishnan (1888-1975) Bhagavat Geeta
(d) Leonardo Davinci (1452-1509) Mona Lisa
(e) J.S. Mill (1806-1873) Principles of Political Economy
(f) J.J. Rousseau (1712-1778) Confessions
(g) Edward Gibbon (1737-1794) Decline and fall of Roman Empire
(h) Jawharlal Nehru (1889-1964) Discovery of India
(i) Bertrand Russell (1872-1970) Marriage and Morals
(j) W.A. Mozart (1756-1761) Marriage of Figaro

6.9 FAVOURED CATEGORY DEVICE (FCD)

It means the classes in array may be arranged in the sequence of decreasing quantity of published documents in them. This Principle is also known as Principle of Literary warrant, and the term 'Literary warrant' was introduced by Wyndham Hulme. It means the quantity of publications available on the subject. The subjects having relativity by large number of publications on them may be treated as favoured subjects in any array of classes, when no other principle will arrange them in more helpful sequence.

For example in (MC) J Agriculture the division 38 seed (i.e.

seed as food) and its divisions are arranged on the basis of this principle. Rice J 381 having greater literary warrant is listed first followed by Wheat, Oat, Rye etc. The other isolates under 38 are arranged in the decreasing sequence of their literary warrant. Here is an example from J Agriculture.

J38	Seed
J381	Rice
J382	Wheat
J383	Oat
J384	Rye
J385	Corn
J386	Barley
J387	Millet

The same principle might have been followed in the listing of domesticated animals under [P] of K Animal Husbandry, the divisions under 31 secretion is further divided by 311 cow, 312 buffalo and 313 she goat. The application of this device needs care and judgment.

6.10 SUMMARY

Universe of knowledge is dynamic, ever growing, multi dimensional and multi faceted. As a result, new subject come into existence which call for formation of new isolates or sharpening existing isolates in the scheme for Library Classification. Colon Classification employed eight devices: 1. Chronological, 2. Geographical, 3. Subject, 4. Mnemonic, 5. Alphabetical, 6. Super Imposition, 7. Classic and, 8. Favoured Category to sharpen the focus of any facet.

Chronological Device (CD) means using chronological number as an isolate number or adding to host class number a chronological number. Geographical Device (GD) consists of using geographical number or adding to host number geographical number. Subject Device (SD) consists of using class number as a isolate number or adding to host isolate number a class number. Mnemonic Device (MD) consists in choosing the digit for further division of a class i.e. formation or sharpening of a focus. Seminal Mnemonics means using the same digit to represent seminally equivalent concepts with different terms. Alphabetical Device (AD) consists of using the first or the first two or first three initial letters of an international name of an isolate term or adding similarly to a host number. Super Imposition Device (SID) means sharpening a focus in the form of an isolate by restricting its extension to the portion of it falling within another isolate of the same facet. Classic Device (CLD) is employed for bringing together the different editions of a classic in a class, the different editions and commentaries and sub-commentaries on the said classic at one place. Favoured Category Device (FCD) means arranging classes in an array on the basis of decreasing quality of published documents on them. This is also known as 'Principle of Literary Warrant'.

These devices help to achieve autonomy to the classifier, which is the bedrock of Colon Classification

6.11 KEY WORDS

ALPHABETICAL DEVICE: Device of using the first or the first two or the first three etc. initial letters of an international name of an isolate term and adding to a host number.

CHRONOLOGICAL DEVICE: Device of using a chronological numbers as an isolate number or adding to a host isolate number a chronological number.

CLASSIC DEVICE: Device of bringing together the different editions of a classic in a class, the different editions of each of its commentaries and sub commentaries on the host book.

FAVOURED CATEGORY DEVICE: Device of arranging classes in an array in the sequence of decreasing quantity of published documents.

GEOGRAPHICAL DEVICE: Device of using geographical number or adding to host isolate number a geographical number.

MNEMONIC DEVICE: Device consists of choosing the digit for further division of a class i.e. the formation or sharpening of a focus in regard to different possible significance's of digits available for use.

SUBJECT DEVICE: Device of using class numbers as an isolate number or adding to a host isolate number a class number.

SUPER IMPOSITION DEVICE: Device of pre-fixing a connecting symbol between tow isolate numbers representing the isolate ideas from the same facet.

6.12 ANSWERS TO SELF CHECK EXERCISES

Exercise-1

(a) 2m73,N98

(b) 2:51M76

(c) 0111,3M35,1

(d) V44:51y7M69,1

(e) 2p44,N98

(f) Q290M8;5

(g) ND5,F:9

(h) T15:5,1NB

(i) SM9,65:526

(j) C5:38N28

Exercise-2

(a) V44:19 (zk)

(b) Z56,3

(c) R855

(d) P35,9D4416

(e) NA441,G92

(f) NB44,J3

(g) E9Gm44,N99

(h) Y33-773:5

(i) A14,156'N97

(j) 1:8ml,N90]

Exercise-3

(a) 24(F)

(b) D6,8(MD13)

(c) NA56,9(A,f)

(d) ND44,9(Q2)

(e) R4,(Q3)

(f) T4:2(2)

(g) V44:58(L:5)

(h) X8(F1823):95854

(i) H(G:2)

(j) Y:411:5(4)

Exercise-4

(a) 22:8:7

(b) 035:5:g

(c) N;6.44 or N44:6

(d) V44,1:3:3

(e) Q:4:4

(f) F:2

(g) Y744:1:1 or Y:1:1.44

(h) J381:6:4

(i) MY2:8

(j) a,7:7

Exercise-5

(a) KZ331J:71

(b) 032,1M78

(c) J382B

(d) D5135HH

(e) D6,8(M31)BPL

(f) T.4416,e4,AV

(g) K96.44,g,OS

(h) J.441.glk

(i) NQ44xSG

(j) D66e3S

Exercise-6

(a) R855xL24,1

(b) U8.1xM25,1

(c) R65,6xM88,1

(d) NQ52x152,1

(e) XxN06,1

(f) WxL12,1

(g) V1-52xL37,

(h) V44xM89,1

(i) R42xM72,1

(j) NR5931xK56,1

(Note: In the work facet the digit 1 has been added treating the work of each author as his first work)

6.13 ASSIGNMENT

Assign Class Numbers to the following titles:

1. Marketing problems of Cotton growers
2. India: Irrigation Management
3. From farm house to Rastrapathi Bhavan: Biography of President Sanjeeva Reddy
4. Poverty and development in India villages
5. Management of Agricultural Research
6. Philosophical issues in Journalism
7. Indian Architecture: Problems in interpretation of 18th and 19th century Architecture
8. Intellectual property rights
9. Moghul monument in the Pubjab and Haryana
10. Plants in Indian Temple Art
11. International Labour organization (Estd.1919)

12. A guide to curriculum review for basic nursing education
13. Environmental Geomorphology
14. Proceedings of the National Seminar on Technology trends in Oil
15. Administrative History of British India'

6.14 SUGGESTED READINGS

1. Navlani, K and Gidwani, NN. 1981. *A practical guide to colon classification*. Oxford IBH Publishing Co. New Delhi
2. Raju, AAN.1984. *Decimal, Universal Decimal Colon Classification, a study in composition*, Ajanta Publications, Delhi
3. Ranganathan, SR. 1960. *Colon Classification* 6th Edition Aisa Publishing House, Bombay
4. Sachdeva, MS 1983. *Colon Classification Theory and Practice*, 2nd Edn Reprint Sterling publishers, New Delhi
5. Satija, MP, 1984. *Manual of Practical Colon Classification* Sterling Publishers, New Delhi

UNIT 7

Differential Facets, Parallel Schedules And Telescoped Facets

7.0 OBJECTIVES

In the previous unit we have introduce you to different devices employed in CC to achieve coextensive class number. In this unit we will introduced you to Differential Facets, Parallel Schedules and Telescoped Facets. After going through this unit you will be able to:

- Understand the concept and meaning of Differential Facets, Parallel Schedules and Telescoped Facets
- Know the application of these three notational techniques viz. Differential Facets, Parallel Schedules and Telescoped array in CC and the place of their occurrence in the schedules of CC
- Grasp the advantages of these three techniques and their role in achieving coextensive class number, and
- Understand the concept of Telescoped array and its application in CC

7.1 INTRODUCTION

In CC we find that in some main classes the whole preceeding facet qualifies each focus of facet. For Example in 2 Library Science

(MC) we find that each focus in Personality [P] facet is qualified by the whole of problem facet i.e. [E] [2P]. But in certain (MCs) each focus in a facet is not qualified by the whole of preceedings facet. That is different foci in the same facet require different facets to qualify them. For example in the (MC) D Engineering the foci in [P] i.e. Irrigation, Building, Road, Railways, and Airways etc. are qualified by different foci in [P2] facet. That is foci in [P2] facet is not common to all foci in [P1] facet. Such occurrence is common in the schedules of CC because the features of each subject are not alike and hence foci also differs. This is the case in respect of [E] facet of some (MCs). This type of facets is called differential facets. These differential facets act as special isolates to meet the increasing specialization indifferent fields especially in Science and Technology and help to achieve coextensive class number.

In CC we find that some of the isolates of a particular facet in a particular (MC), may also be borrowed wholly or partially by the another (MC). Let us take for example isolate child. It occurs in the (MCs) S Psychology, T Education and Y Sociology under [P] facet. The personality facets of these three (MCs) are almost the same. Let us take another example. Foci in [E] [2P] given under G Biology is common for I Botany, K Zoology and L Medicine. Like this we find several instances in CC. This leads to parallel schedules or parallel sequence of foci in a facet common to more than one (MC). This is secured with the help of the principle of helpful sequence. These parallel schedules contribute to the emergence of scheduled mnemonics.

Telescoping of facets means the presentation of schedules of all levels as if they are all formed of a single schedule. It also means different facets in the idea plane appear to be telescoped into a single schedule in the notational plane. A subject may present different levels of the same fundamental category in one and the same round. We also find telescoped array in CC. It means array of classes in a schedule of classification made of coordinate and subordinate isolates, as viewed from the idea plane, but whose class numbers appear to be coordinate as viewed from the notational plane.

These three notational techniques i.e. Differential Facets, Parallel Schedules and Telescoped Facets have greatly contributed to achieve coextensive class numbers. These three techniques are presented below with suitable worked out examples.

7.2 DIFFERENTIAL FACET

As we told to you in the introduction, the isolates in one facet denoting specialized articles may combined only with a particular isolate from another facet. The secondary facet having a limited combining capacity is called differential facet i.e. they differ from isolate to isolate. In CC different foci in the same facet require different facets to qualify them. For example in the (MC) Z Law, property and contract are foci in[P2] facet, [P1] is community concerned i.e. for example India, UK etc. The various features of each focus constitute [P3] facet. But the features needed to qualify Law of property are different from those needed to qualify Law of contract. So [P3] facet for property (Ownership, Possession, Landlord, Tenant etc) is quite different from [P3] facet for contract (Capacity, consideration, formation etc). Such variant facets are called differential facets. Here are few examples of such differential facets found in some of the (MCs)

7.2.1 D Engineering

In the (MC) D Engineering, the foci in Part [P2], would depend upon the work Division [P] and would be different for different types of work.

Here are Few Worked Out Examples

1. Flood proteticing for river training work D26,8
2. Building Foundation D3,2
3. Window of Railway Carriage D5153,67
4. Television D65,45
5. Overhead transmission of Electricity D66,21

7.2.2 E Chemistry

In the (MC) E chemistry, Foci in [P2] for substance numbers 5,6,7 and 8 in [P] are only provided. Here are few worked out examples.

1. Starch Compound E6892,8
2. Sluphur ring compound E86,6
3. Organic acid E5,3
4. Olefin ether E63,383
5. Derivative acid in cellulose E6894,38

7.2.3 J Agriculture

In (MC) J Agriculture [2P] for foci in[E] and [2E] for foci in [E] are differently given. That is foci in [2P] and [2E] are different for different foci in [E]. Here are few worked out examples.

1. Conservation of Soil J:1:7
2. Application of phosphate manure J:242:3
   NOTE: Here 42 is [2P] and: 3 is [2E]
3. Transplanting of seeds J:38:5
   NOTE: Here 8 is [2P] from part Array of [P] and:5 is [2E]
4. Harvesting of flowers J:76
   NOTE: Here 6 is [2P] from part array of [P]
5. Cold storage of fruits J:77:84
   NOTE: Here 7 is [2P] from part array of [P] and : 84 is [2E] cum [3P] for 7 of [E]

7.2.4 KZ Animal Husbandry

Like J Agriculture in KZ Animal husbandry also we find the use of differential facets. Here are few worked out examples.

1. Cow Milk KZ311:71
   NOTE: Here 1 is [2P] for 31 of [P] for 7 Harvest of [E]. Without using 7 we cannot use 1.
2. Buffalo Ghee KZ312:74
   NOTE: Here 4 is [2P] for 31 of [2P] for 7 Harvest of [E]
3. Feeding leaves to Goat KZ331:1 (J25)
4. Fowl eggs KZ351:75
5. Cold Storage of Cow Butter Milk KZ311:754:84

As per direction Foci in [2E] cum [3P] for 7 of [E] is to be taken from J Agriculture.

7.2.5 T Education

In T Education foci in [2P2] is different for different foci [E] [2P] viz: 3 Teaching Techniques, 4 Students work, 5 Education Measurement. Here are few worked out examples.

1. Audio visual method of teaching chemistry T:3[E],1
2. Home work for school students T2:4,1
3. University Examinations T4:5,5
4. Library work for Intermediate students T25:4,2
5. Lecture method of teaching Political Science at P.G Level T45:3 (W),97

7.2.6 X Economics

In the (MC) X Economics [M] is exclusively provided for [P] money. Like wise 62 Bank and 72 Taxation in [P] have few different Energy Isolates. These two have to be exclusively used for 62 and 72 of [P]. Here are few worked out examples.

1. Rate of interest in foreign Banks X6295:11
2. Exemption of Income Tax X724:2
3. Paper Currency X61:4
4. Effect of Indirect Tax X729:5
5. Cheque facility in Saving Bank X627:5

7.2.7 Y Sociology

In the (MC) Y Sociology for foci in [E] [2P] i.e. 1 Culture, 3 Activity, 7 Personality and 8 Equipment 4 social Pathology and 5 Demography, different [2E] [3P] isolates is separately provided. Here are few worked out examples:

1. Influence of culture Y:1:5
2. Improvement of rural personality Y31:7:7
3. Diagnosis of Intemperance Y:4:3
4. Earthquake relief work Y:436:67
5. Control of over population Y:5:6

NOTE: Without first using appropriate focus from [E] [2P], we cannot directly use focus from [2E][3P].

7.2.8 Z Law

In the (MC) Z Law foci in [P3] varies for foci in [P2]. Similarly foci in [P4] is separately given for 7 judgement and decree in [P3]. Here are few worked out examples.

1. Law of ownership of property Z,211,1
2. Illegal mortgage Z,331,4
3. Biographical sketches of Supreme Court Judge of India Z44,81,11,w
4. Admissability of Oral evidence Z,94,3
5. Injunction to expert decree in Criminal Proceedings Z,75,73,5

Self check Exericse-1

(a) Lubrication of general machinery
(b) Design of Nuclear reactors
(c) Synthesis in volumetric chemistry
(d) Application of organic manure for tobacco
(e) Annual yield of flowers
(f) Storing root feed for pigs
(g) Teaching history through mother tongue in secondary schools
(h) Incidence of stamp duty
(i) Famine relief work in rural areas
(j) Limited ownership of land property in India

7.3 PARALLEL SCHEDULES

In CC we find the use of one and the same digit or digit group to represent an isolate idea or an array isolate idea, in more than one subject. This method leads to the emergence of scheduled mnemonics. In CC it has been estimated that there are seventy six cases of parallel schedules. The parallel schedules secure conformity to the canon of consistent sequence and satisfy law of parsimony in regard to length of schedules of classification. In all these seventy six cases we find that the schedules of isolates will be parallel in the sense that the isolate terms and their respective isolates numbers will be the same in all those cases. Here is an example of parallel schedule.

Psychology	Education	Sociology
[P]	[P]	[P]
Child	Pre-Secondary	Groups arising
New born		from age and sex
Toddler	Pre-School	Child
Infant	Elementary	
Pre-adolescent	Secondary	Youth
Adolescent	Adult	Old Person
↓	↓	↓

The following subsections deal with important examples of parallel schedules as found in CC.

7.3.1 2 Library Science

In the (MC) 2 Library Science the foci for (M) facet is same as foci in [P] for a General Bibliography.

1. Lending of Periodicals in University Libraries 234:46:62
2. Maintenance of Manuscripts in Religious Libraries 24 (Q):12:88
3. Classification of Patents in Commercial Libraries 245:48:51

NOTE: In all the three examples, 46,12 and 48 were taken from [P] of a Gineralia Bibliography

7.3.2 C9B3 Nucleus

In C9 B3 Nucleus, the foci in [E] cum [2P] is similar to those for C5 Radiation

1. Propagation of cosmic ray C9B38:2
2. Dispersion of Proton C9B35:3
3. Effects of Cosmic ray C9B38:38

NOTE: In the above three worked out examples 2,3 and 38 were taken from foci in [E] [2P] of C5 Radiation.

7.3.3 F Technology

In F Technology foci in [P] is same as in E Chemistry. Like

wise foci in [E] [2P] is same as problem division of 8 Manipulation of (MCs) E Chemistry.

1. Fatigue study of Iron F182:94 (~~8~~94)
2. Crystallization of Salt F4:31 (~~8~~31)
3. Fermentation of Starch F6892:7 (~~8~~7)

NOTE: As per rule F22 (P1.77) the second digit onwards in the subdivision of problem division 8 Manipulation of (MC) E Chemistry should be used. Therefore the initial digit 8 under [E] facet is dropped.

7.3.4 I Botany and K Zoology

Foci in [E] cum [2P] for the (MCs) I Botany and K Zoology are same as foci in [E] cum [2P] of G Biology.

1. Plant pathology I:4
2. Animal Physiology K:3
3. Migration of Birds K96:58
4. Prevention of disease in flowering plants I5:4:5

NOTE: As per instruction under 4 pathology (P2.52) further divisions have to be taken from L Medicine. Where ever necessary foci in [2E] cum [3P] for 4 of [E] can be taken from L Medicine. Hence: 5 is taken from [2E] cum [3P] of L Medicine.

7.3.5 NB Town Planning and NQ Painting

Foci in [E] for B Town Planning are same as foci in [E] of NA Architecture. Similarly foci in [P3] for NQ painting are a same as foci in [P3] for ND sculpture.

1. Location of play grounds in cities NB,5,65:1
2. Models of Market place in towns NB,3,5:8
3. Painting of Landscape NQ,3
4. Painting of animals on wood NQ,5;1

7.3.6 S Psychology and Y Sociology

In these two (MCs) we find occurrence of parallel schedules at several points in the schedules. Some of them are cited below:

The digit 8under [P] of (MC) S Psychology is Social

Psychology. This is to be divided as [P] of Y Sociology. The digit 1 under [E] cum [2P] of Y Sociology is Nervous System. This is to be divided as [P] 7 L Medicine.

The digit 2 in [P] of Y Sociology is Family. This is be further divides in R4 Ethics.

The digit 6 in [P] of Y sociology is Abnormal and defective. This is to be subdivided as in S Psychology. The digit 3 in [E] cm [2P] of Y Sociology are Transport-Track and Transport-Vehicle. These two isolates have to be divided as 4 of [P] and 5 of [P] of Engineering. Here are few worked out examples.

1. Psychology of friendly society S83 (Taken from 83 of [P] of Y Sociology)
2. Psychological reaction of Brain S12 (Taken from 72 of [P] of L Medicine)
3. Sociology of Genius Y61 (Taken from 61 of [P] of S Psychology)
4. Hindu Marriage activity Y73 (Q2):317 (Taken from 217 of [P] of R4 Ethics)
5. Rural Country Cart Y31:85121 (Taken from 5121 of (P) of D5 Engineering)

7.3.7 V History and W Political Science

In (MC) History the focus 512 Liberty of Family in foci [E] [2P] is to be divided as [P2] 12 of Z law. The foci in [P2] and [E] cum [2P] is same as for V History. Here are few worked out examples.

1. Liberty of Husband and wife V44:51221 (Taken from 1221 of [P2] of Z Law
2. Liberty of Marriage in China V51:5122 (Taken from 122 of [P] of Z Law)
3. Functions of Political parties in a Democracy W6, 4:3

   Note : Here focus 4[P2] and 3[E][2P] is taken from V History
4. Disarmament policy W:19(zT)

   Note: Here the focus 19 (zT) [E] cum [2P] is taken from V History

5. Freedom of Public meeting in a Dictatorship W64:54
   Note : Here focus 54 [E] cum [2P] is taken from V History

Self Check Exercise-2

(a) Cataloguing of maps in Cartographic Libraries
(b) Catalysis of Alkaloid
(c) Control of diseases of rose plants
(d) Fasting in mammals
(e) Perspective plan of parks in metropolises
(f) Preservation of landscape paintings in canvas
(g) Psychology of personality of Military class
(h) Asylum for sick and infirm in India
(i) Liberty of marriage in USA
(j) Freedom of association in a democracy

7.4 TELESCOPED FACETS

Telescoped facets is defined as "array of isolates in a schedule of classification made of isolates belonging to different facets, favouring consecutive levels in the same round of manifestation of one and the same fundamental category, as viewed from the idea plane, but whose isolate numbers appear to be all coordinate ones as viewed form the notational plane".

By telescoping of facets we mean the presentation of schedules of all levels of a fundamental category, as if they formed a single schedule. A subject may present different levels of the same fundamental category in one and the same round. The telescoping of facets has two advantages viz. 1. Naming of different levels of schedules of the same fundamental category is made absolute such as level 1, level 2 level 3 and so on. They are named relatively to one another with the use of epithet 'earlier'. 2. If a subject does not present some intermediate levels, the isolate number belonging to them need not find a place in the class number.

This notational technique is possible when notation is a mixed one. This is widely used in CC. Here is an example of how this technique is employed in CC in (MC) Economic under [E] personal management9.

4 = Safety measure (94)

9D = Semi skilled personnel (after telescoping point 1) (99D)

↓

J6 = Immigrant personnel (9J6) (After telescoping point 2).

Let us consider the following class numbers.

X:9J6, 9D, 4 = Safety measures of immigrant semi skilled personnel.

Here it is clear that J6 = In migrant personnel is an isolate in the first level personality facet in the second round.

9D = Semi skilled personnel is an isolate in the second level personality facet

4 = Safety measure is an isolate in the third level personality facet

This is as viewed from the idea plane. But the example cited above from the schedule, the three isolates appear to belong to one and the same facet as viewed from the notation plane. Here are few more worked out examples.

1. Social Security for married technical staff X:9F5,9T,58
2. Housing services for urban administrative staff X:9H5,9V,62
3. Profit sharing for apprentice semi skilled staff X:9N3,9D,36

7.5 TELESCOPED ARRAY

Telescoped array is defined as 'array of isolate in a schedules of classification, made of coordinate and subordinate classes as viewed form the idea plane, but whose isolate numbers appear to be coordinate as viewed form the notational plane'. It means presentation of the isolates obtained on the basis of different characteristics in the same array as the one presenting the characteristics themselves as Quasi Isolates. Here are examples of telescoped arrays cited from CC.

7.5.1 I Botany Foci in [P]

1. Cryptogrammia
2. Thallophyta

3. Bryophyta
4. Petridophyta
5. Phanerogamia
6. Gymnosperm
7. Monocotyledon
8. Dictoyledon

Here cryptogamia and phanerogamia belong to array of order 1, and all other isolates belong to array of order 2 as view from the idea plane. But as viewed from the notational plane both the groups of isolates appear to belong to array of order 1 in CC. Here is another example:

7.5.2 Telescoped array of Geographical Divisions

1. World

Tel (A2) into (A1) Begins

4. Asia
5. Europe
6. Africa
7. America
8. Australia

Tel (A2) into (A1) ends

As viewed form the idea plane 'World' as a whole is the only class of order1. There cannot be any other class of that order. Thus the digits after '1 World fall vacant. In the above example the other digits 4-8have been used to represent the continents of the World. But as viewed from the idea plane the continents are classes of order 2. But in the above exempla the World and the Continents appear to be classes of the same order viz. Order 1 as viewed form the notational plane.

Here are few worked out examples:

1. Defence Policy of Australia V8:19 (zP)
2. Physiology of Gymnosperm I6:3
3. Classification of Vertebrate K9:515

Self check Exercise-3

(a) Unemployment benefit for unskilled disabled workers

(b) Adjudication of strike by Trade Unions

(c) Arbitration of strained relations by Employer union

(d) Negotiation of lockout in large scale Iron Industry

(e) Ecology of sea weeds

(f) Physiology of tissues of malvales

(g) Mutation in seeds

(h) Migration of amphibians

(i) Natural history of birds

(j) Social conditions in Russia

7.6 SUMMARY

In CC we find that in certain (MCs) each focus in a fact is not qualified by the whole of preceeding facet. For example in the (MC) D Engineering the foci in [P] i.e. Irrigation, Building, Road, Railways, and Airways etc are qualified by different foci in [P2] facet. This type of facets is called differential facets. These act, as special isolates to meet the increasing demand of specialization in different fields of human endeavor.

In CC we also find that some of the isolates of particular facet in a particular (MC) may also be borrowed wholly or partially by another (MC). Take for example the isolate child. It occurs in the (MCs) S Psychology, T Education and Y Sociology as [P] facet.

The foci in [P] facet of these three (MCs) are almost the same. Like this we find common Energy Facet for the (MCs) G Biology, I Botany, K Zoology and L Medicine. This leads to the emergence of parallel sequence or parallel schedules. This phenomenon automatically conforms to the emergence of scheduled mnemonics.

Telescoping of facets means the presentation of schedules of all levels of as if they are all formed of a single schedule. It also means different facets in the idea plane appear to be telescoped in to a single schedule in the notational plane. We also find telescoped array in CC. It means array of classes in a schedule of classification made of coordinate and subordinate isolates as viewed form the idea plane, but whose class numbers appear to be coordinate as viewed the notational plane. These three notational techniques have greatly contributed to achieve coextensive class number in CC.

7.7 KEYWORDS

DIFFERENTAL FACET: An Isolate from one facet can be combined with any other isolate from a different facet .

PARALLEL SCHEDULE: The use of one and the same digit or digit group to represent an isolate idea or an array isolate idea in more than one subject.

TELESCOPED ARRAY: Array of isolates in a schedule of classification made of coordinate and subordinate isolates as viewed from the idea plane, but whose isolate numbers appear to be coordinate as viewed from the notational plane.

TELESCOPED FACET: Array of isolates in a schedule of classification made of isolates belonging to different facets as viewed from the idea of plane, but whose isolate numbers appear to be coordinate ones as viewed from the notational plane.

7.8 ANSWERS TO SELF CHECK EXERCISES

Exercise-1

(a) D627,7

(b) D7,13:4

(c) E:3,4

(d) J452:25:3

(e) J:76:7,

(f) J334:1(J53):8

(g) J2:3(V),31

(h) X7292:1

(i) Y31:4353:67

(j) Z44,211,14

Exercise-2

(a) 2:4 (V11):55

(b) E92:8

(c) I8331:4:5

(d) K97:346

(e) NB44,7,66:6

(f) NQ,3:7:98

(g) S854:7

(h) Y64:4:65

(i) Z73:5122

(j) W6:58(y8)

Exercise-3

(a) X:9P4,9C,5851

(b) X:97D,9D,7

(c) X:97W,9A,6

(d) X8(F182)''979W,3

(e) I22:5

(f) I816,12:63

(g) I,178:63

(h) K93:58

(i) K96:12

(j) Y.58

7.9 ASSIGNMENT

Assign Class Numbers to the following titles:

1. Specification of Machine Tools
2. Physical analysis of Cellulose
3. Transplanting of coconut
4. Preservation of duck eggs
5. Field work for research students
6. Rate of interest in mortgage bank
7. Cement roads in rural areas of Andhra Pradesh
8. Maintenance of film rolls in Research Libraries

9. Industrial biochemistry
10. Plant genetics
11. Animal evolution
12. Prevention of blindness in rural areas of U.P.

7.10 SUGGESTED READINGS

1. Raju, AAN 1984. *Decimal, Universal Decimal and Colon Classification, a study in comparison*, Ajanta Publications, Delhi
2. Ranganathan, SR. 1967. *Prolegomena to Library Classification* 3rd Edition, Asia Publishing House, Bombay
3. ———————— 1960. *Colon Classification* 6th Edition Asia Publishing House, Bombay
4. Sachdeva, MS. 1983. *Colon Classification, Theory and Practice.* 2nd Edition reprint Sterling Publishers, New Delhi
5. Satija, M.P. 1984. *Manual of Practical Colon Classification*, Sterling Publishers, New Delhi.

BLOCK 3
Practical Classification

This block introduces you to application of schedules given under different main classes (MCs) in CC well supported by quoting relevant rules from part I of CC. This block consists of the following five units (8-12).

UNIT 8: Covers the main classes under mathematical and physical sciences, which include B Mathematics, C Physics, D Engineering, E Chemistry and F Technology. The facet formula provided for each of the (MC) is explained and the use of schedules in the construction of class number is amply demonstrated with suitable worked out examples.

UNIT 9: Covers the main classes under Biological sciences, which include G Biology, H Geology, HX Mining, I Botany, J Agriculture, K Zoology, KX Animal Husbandry and L Medicine. The facet formula provided for each of the (M) is explained and the use of schedules in the construction of class number is clearly demonstrated with suitable worked out examples.

UNIT10: Covers the main classes under Humanities which include N fine Arts, O Literature, P Linguistics, Q Religion and R Philosophy. The facet formula provided for each of the (MC) is explained and the use of schedules in construction of class number is presented with suitable worked out examples.

UNIT11: Covers the main classes under Social Sciences, which include T Education, U Geography, V History, W Political Science, X Economics, Y Sociology and Z law. The facet formula provided for each of the (MC) is explained and the application of schedules in the construction of class number is demonstrated with suitable worked out examples.

UNIT12: Covers the remaining main classes which include a General Bibliography, 2 Library Science, M Useful Arts. Δ

Spiritual Experience and Mysticism.

The facet formula provided for each of the (MC) is explained and the use of schedules in the construction of class number is amply demonstrated with suitable worked out examples.

UNIT 8

Main Classes Under Mathematical and Physical Sciences

0 OBJECTIVES

In the previous units i.e. 1-7 (Blocks 1 and 2) you have been introduced to the theoretical aspects of Colon Classification. In this unit we will introduce you to the art of practical classification with CC. After going through this unit you should be able to:

- Understand the rules of classification pertaining to Mathematical and Physical Sciences.
- Know the facet formula of each of the main class and its implications; and
- Assign class numbers to titles falling under the (MCs) B Mathematics, C Physics, D Engineering, E Chemistry and F Technology.

8.1 INTRODUCTION

In the first two blocks viz. 1 Theory of Colon Classification and 2. Towards coextensive class number we have introduced you to various theoretical aspects of CC. These theoretical aspects with relevant rules and worked out examples have been introduced to you through the units 1-7. This unit introduces you to the art of practical classification.

In this unit we will introduce you to the (MCs) falling under Mathematical and Physical Sciences. Please refer to Chapter 1 (P2.4) of the schedules for list of (MCs). The (MCs) which fall under Mathematical and Physical Sciences are: B Mathematics, C Physics, D Engineering, E Chemistry and F Technology. Each (MC) will be introduced to you citing the facet formula and important and relevant rules from part 1 of CC and well supported by worked out examples. Let us take up each of these (MCs).

8.2 B MATHEMATICS

"The science of numbers and their operations, inter relations, combinations, generalizations and abstractions and of space configurations and their structure, measurement, transformations and generalizations''

It is further divided on canonical lines such as:

B1 Arithmatic

B2 Algebra

B3 Analysis

B4 Other Methods

B5 Trigonometry

B6 Geometry

B7 Mechanics

B8 Physico-Mathematics

B9 Astronomy

For some of the Canonical divisions we find facet formula and their implications are explained in theory part (P1.66-1.69) with some worked out examples. You should be familiar with the relevant rules given in the theory part. Here are few worked out examples for some of the important Canonical divisions.

8.2.1 B13 Integer (Theory of Numbers)

The facet formula for B13 is as follows:

B13 [P], [P2]: [E]

Where [P] = Number
[P2] = Theory
[E] = Method

1. Gold bach' theorem

Analysis

Integer (CNC) = B13

Gold bach's theorem [P], 5L

Synthesis

B13 +, 5L = B13, 5L

2. Algebraic methods of distribution of prime numbers

Analysis

Integer (CNC) = B13

Prime Number [P] = 1

Distribution [P2] = ,2

Algebraic method [E] cum [2P]:2

Synthesis

B13+1+2,+:2 = B13 1,2:2

3. Geometrical method of multiplicative function

Analysis

Integer = B13 (CNC)

Multiplicative function = 9N [P2]

Geometrical method = :6 [E] Cum [2P]

Synthesis

B13 +, 9N + :6 = B13,9N:6

8.2.2 B25 Higher Algebra

The facet formula for B25 is as follows.

B 25 [P], [P2]:[E] [2P]

Where [P] = Form

[P2] = Degree

[E] [2P] = Transformation

1. Binary linear special invariant

Analysis

Higher Algebra = B25 (CNC)

Binary = 2 [P]

Linear = , 1 [P2]

Special Invariant = : 18[E] [2P]

Synthesis

B25 + 2 +,1 + 18 = B252, 1:18

2. Linear Transformation of nth degree quaternary

Analysis

Higher = B25 (CNC)

Quaternary = 4 [P]

nth degree = ,7 [P2]

Linear transformation = :1[E] [2P]

Synthesis

B25 + 4 ,7 + :1 = B254, 7:1

3. Ternary Special transformation

Analysis

Higher Algebra = B25(CNC)

Ternary = 3 [P]

Special Transformation= :8[E] [2P]

Synthesis

B25 + 3 + :8 = B253 : 8

8.2.3 B33 Differential And Integral Equation

The facet formula for B33 is as follows:

B33 [P[, [P2], [P3]: [E] [2P]

Where

[P] = Equation

[P2] = Degree

[P3] = Order

[E] [2P] = Problem

1. Formal solution of simultaneous quadratic differential first order equations

Analysis

Differential Equation = B33 (CNC)

Simultaneous = 2[P]

Quadratic = ,2 [P2]

First Order = ,1 [P3]

Formal solution = :5 [E] [2P]

Synthesis

B33 + 2 + ,2 + ,1+ :5 = B332,2,1:5

2. Algebraic theory of partial cubic differential third order equation

Analysis

Differential Equation = B33 (CNC)

Partial = 4 [P]

Cubic = ,3 [P2]

Third Order = ,3 [P3]

Algebraic theory = :52 [E] [2P]

Synthesis

B33 + 4 ++ ,3 + ,3 + :52 = B334, 3, 3:52

8.2.4 B6 Geometry

The facet formula for B6 is as follows:

B6 [P]:[E] [2P]

Where [P] = Space

[E][2P] = Method

1.Descriptive line geometry

Analysis

Geometry = B6 (CNC)

Line = 1 [P]

Descriptive = :5 [E] [2P]

Synthesis

B6 + 1 + :5 = B61:5

2. Practical plane geometry

Analysis

Geometry = B6 (CNC0

Plane = 2 {P}

Practical = :4 [E] [2P]

Synthesis

B6 + 2 + :4 = B62:4

3. Higher differential cubic geometry

Analysis

Geometry = B6 (CNC)

Cubic = 33 [P]

Higher differential = :35[E] [2P]

Synthesis

B6 + 33 + :35 = B633:35

8.2.5 B7 Mechanics

The facet formula for B7 is as follows:

B7 [P]:[E] [2P]

Where [P] = Problem

[E] [2P] = Problem

1. Dynamics of solids

Analysis

Mechanics = B7 (CNC)

Solids = 1 [P]

Dynamics = :3[E] [2P]

Synthesis

B7 + 5 + :353 = B75 : 353

2. Vibration of viscous

Analysis

Mechanics = B7 (CNC)

Viscous = 56 [P]

Vibration = :5[E] [2P]

Synthesis

B7 + 56 + :5 = B756:5

8.2.6 B9 Astronomy

The facet formula for B9 Astronomy is as follows:

B9 [P] : [E] [2P]

Where[P] = Body

[E] [2P] = Problem

1. Lunar Eclipse

Analysis

Astronomy = B9 (CNC)

Moon (Lunar) = 2[P]

Eclipse = :57 [E} [2P]

Synthesis

B9 + 2 + :57 = B92: 57

2. Orbit of Earth

Analysis

Astronomy = B9 (CNC)

Earth = 1[P]

Orbit = :72 [E] [2P]

Synthesis

B9 + 1 + :72 = B91 : 7

3. Distance of sun

Analysis

Astronomy = B9 (CNC)

Sun = 2 [P]

Distance = :624[E] [2P]

Synthesis

B0 + 3 + :624 = B93 : 624

Self Check Exercise-1

(a) The story of solar system

(b) Introduction to coordinate geometry

(c) Functions of complex variable

(d) Non-Euclidean Plane Geometry

(e) Dyuloka, a journal of Indian Astronomical Association, 1997

(f) Total solar eclipse in India in 1998

(g) Annual report of the Director of Royal Astronomical Observatory, Greenvich, 1996

(h) Statistics for Cost-Accountants

(i) Biography of Nicolaus Copernicus (1473-1543)

(j) Comparative study of constitution of Mars and Jupiter

8.3 C PHYSICS

"A science that deals with matter and energy and their actions in the fields of Mechanics, Acoustics, Optics, Heat, Electricity, Magnetism, Radiation, Atomic structure and Nuclear Phenomena''. It is further divided on Canonical lines such as:

1 Fundamentals

C2 Properties of Matter

C3 Sound

C4 Heat

C5 Light, Radiation

C6 Electricity

C7 Magnetism

C8 Cosmic hypothesis

For some of the canonical divisions we find facet formula and their implications are explained in the theory part under chapter 5 (Pl.70 – 1.71) with some worked out examples. We should be familiar with the rules and explanation, which will help us in classifying documents falling under C Physics. Here are few worked out examples for some of the important canonical divisions.

8.3.1 C2 Properties of Matter

The facet formula for C2 is as follows

C2 [P]:[E] [2P]

Where [P] = State
[E] [2P] = Problem

1. Pressure of gas

Analysis

Properties of Matter = C2 (CNC)
Gas = 8 [P]
Pressure = :7[E] [2P]

Synthesis

C2 + 8 + :7 = C28:7

2. Diffusion of liquid

Analysis

Properties of Matter = C2 (CNC)
Liquid = 5 [P]
Diffusion = :93 [E] [2P]

Synthesis

C2 + 5 + :93 = C25 :93

3. Shape of Crystals

Analysis

Properties of Matter = C2 (CNC)
Crystal = 16 [P]
Shape = :25

Synthesis

C2 + 16 + :25 = C216:25

8.3.2 C3 Sound

The facet formula for C3 is as follows:

C3 [P]:[E] [2P]

Where [P] = Wave length

[E] [2P] = Problem

1. Propagation of audible sound

Analysis

Sound = C3 (CNC)

Audible sound = 1 [P]

Propagation = :2[E][2P]

Synthesis

C3 + 5 + :8 = C35 :8

8.3.3 C4 Heat

The facet formula for C4 is as follows:

C4 [P]:[E] [2P]

Where [P]= State (To be taken from [P] of C2

[E] [2P] = Problem

Note: In the schedules (P2.37) foci in [P] is not mentioned. But in the theory part (P1.70) under facet formula for C4 Heat, facet [P] represents state (of matter). Therefore it is obvious that foci in [P] for C4 can be taken from foci in [P] of C2 properties of matter.

1. Conduction of heat in solids

Analysis

Heat = C4 (CNC)

Solid = 1[P] Taken from [P] of C2

Conduction = :24 [E] [2P]

Synthesis

C4 + 1+ :24 = C41:24

2. Absorption of heat in liquid

Analysis

Heat = C4 (CNC)

Liquid = 5 [P] taken from [P] of C2

Absorption = :27 [E] [2P]

Synthesis

C4 + 5 +:27 = C45 : 27

3. Change of state of heat in crystal

Analysis

Heat = C4 (CNC)
Crystal = 16 [P] taken from [P] of C2
Change of state = :5[E] [2P]

Synthesis

C4 + 16 + :5 = C416:5

8.3.4 C5 Radiation

The facet formula for C5 is as follows:
C5[P] : [E] [2P]

Where [P] = Wave length
[E] [2P] = Problem

1. Dispersion of light

Analysis

Radiation = C5 (CNC)
Light = 1[P]
Dispersion = :3[E][2P]

Synthesis

C5 + 1+ :3 = C51 :3

2. Effects of X-ray

Analysis

Radiation = C5 (CNC)
X-Ray = 3[P]
Effects = :38[E] [2P]

Synthesis

C5 + 3+ :38 = C53 :38

3. Scattering of ultra violet ray

Analysis

Radiation = C5 (CNC)
Ultra Violet Ray = 2[P]

Scattering = :58 [E] [2P]

Synthesis

C5 + 2+ :58 = C52:58

8.3.5 C6 Electricity

The facet formula for C6 is as follows:

C6 [P] : [E][2P]

Where [P] = Electricity

[E] [2P] = Problem

1. Generation of Current Electricity

Analysis

Electricity = C6 (CNC)

Current = 2 [P]

Generation = :1 [E] [2P]

Synthesis

C6 + 2 + :1 = C62 : 1

2. Potential of statistical electricity

Analysis

Electricity = C6 (CNC)

Statistical = 3[P]

Potential = :3 [E] [2P]

Synthesis

C6 + 3 + :3 = C63: 3

3. Nature of alternate current

Analysis

Electricity = C6 (CNC)

Alternate current = 24 [P]

Nature = :8[E] [2P]

Synthesis

C6 + 24 + :8 = C624 : 8

8:3.6 C7 Magnetism

The facet formula for C7 is as follows:

C7 [P] : [E] [2P]

Where [P] = Magnetism

[E] [2P] = Problem

1. Intensity of diamagnetism

Analysis

Magnetism = C7 (CNC)

Dia = 2 [P]

Intensity = :2 [E][2P]

Synthesis

C7 + 2 + :2 = C72 : 2

2. Nature of ferromagnetism

Analysis

Magnetism = C7 (CNC)

Ferro = 4 [P]

Nature = :8 [E] [2P]

Synthesis

C7 + 4 + :8 = C74 : 8

3. Magnetic surveys in India in 1990

Analysis

Magnetism = C7 (CNC)

India = 44 [S]

1990's = N9 [T]

Survey = t4 (ACI applicable only after time)

Synthesis

C7 + 44 + 'N9 + t4 = C7.44'N9t4

Self check Exercise - 2

(a) Solid state physics

(b) Photometry

(c) Biography of Albert Einstein (1879)

(d) Conduction of heat in solids

(e) Formulas in Physics

(f) Diffraction of Infra red ray

(g) Raman Effect

(h) Annual report of the Director of Bhabha Atomic Research Centre for the year 1998

(i) Analysis guide to experiments in Physics

(j) Line Spectrum according to wave mechanics

8.4 D ENGINEERING

"A science by which the properties of matter and the sources of energy in nature are made useful to man''. The facet formula for D Engineering is as follows:

D[P], [P2]: [E] [2P]

Where [P] = Work

[P2] = Part

[E] [2P] = Problem

1. Rail road engineering in India

Analysis

Engineering = D (MC)

Rail Road = 415 [P]

India = .44 [S]

Synthesis

D + 415 + .44 = D 415.44

2. Railway signaling system

Analysis

Engineering = D (MC)

Rail Road = 415 [P]

Signal = ,94 [P2] for D 415 (Differential facet)

Synthesis

D + 415 + ,94 = D415,94

3. Telegraph Communication Engineering

Analysis

Engineering = D(MC)

Electronics = 65 [P]

Telegraphy = ,47 [P2] for D 65 (Differential facet)

Synthesis

D + 65 + ,47 + D65, 47

4. Overhead transmission of Electricity

Analysis

Engineering = D (MC)

Electrical = 66 [P]

Overhead transmission = ,21 [P2] for D 66 (Differential Facet)

Synthesis

D + 66 + ,21 = D66,21

5. Specifications for heat engines

Analysis

Engineering = D (MC)

Heat = 64 [P]

Engine = ,121 [P2] for 64 Heat (Differential Facet)

Specification = :5[E][2P]

Synthesis

D + 64 + ,121 + :5 = D64, 121: 5

6. Construction of grape crushing machines

Analysis

Engineering = D (MC)

Mechanical = 6 [P]

Crushing Machinery = ,88 [P2] division by [SD]

Grape J387 from [P] of J Agriculture i.e., 88 (J387)

Construction = :7 [E][2P]

Synthesis

D + 6, 88 (J374) + :7 = D6,88(J374): 7

7. Monographs for the design of current meters.

Engineering = D(MC)
Electrical = 66[P]
Current meter = e3 Common isolate

Note: Special common isolate schedule for work facet 66 is provided in the schedule part of Engineering. (P2.45)

Design = :4[E][2P]

Synthesis

D + 66 + e3 + :4 = D 66e3 :4

8. Television in India

Analysis

Engineering = D(MC)
Electronic = 65 [P]
Television = ,45[P2]
India = .44 [S]

Synthesis

D65 + ,45 + .44 = D65, 45.44

Self Check Exercise –3

(a) Design of steel bridge over river Godavari at Rajahmundry (AP)
(b) Cycle repair guide
(c) Execution of Nuclear reactor at Nagarjuna Sagar (AP)
(d) Electrical Purification of water in Hyderabad City
(e) Electric Typewriting machines
(f) Air conditioning of buildings in New Delhi during summer 1998
(g) Application of Thermodynamics for heat engines
(h) Biography of M. Visvesaraya (1861-1962)

(i) Annual report of Karnataka State Electricity Board for the year 1998

(j) A comparative study of Electrical and Electronic Engineering

8.5 E CHEMISTRY

"A science that deals with the composition, structure and properties of substances and of the transformations that they undergo".

The facet formula for E Chemistry is as follows:

E[P], [P2]: [E] [2P]

Where [P] = Substance

[P2] = Combination for 5, 6, 7 and 8 of [P]

[E] [2P] = Problem

8.5.1 Rules

In the schedules (P2.46) we find the facet formula for E Chemistry is a misprint. There is no mention of [P2] facet. In the theory part of chemistry (P1.74) we find an elaborate explanation of various aspects of chemistry schedule. Some of the important rules are quoted below. For proper understanding of theory part one requires knowledge of Chemistry. Some of the important rules are cited below:

The digit 1 and its subdivisions deal with chemistry of specific elements. The classification of elements has been based on periodic table (Rule E 11). Periodic table means an arrangement of chemical elements in order of their atomic numbers in such way to demonstrate the periodic law. Periodic law means the statement that the properties of the elements are in periodic dependence upon their atomic weights, published by Mendelev in 1869. This law is brought out clearly when the elements are arranged in periodic table.

The second digit in the numbers of the subdivisions of substances division represents the group to which the elements belongs and the third digit ordinarily represent the period (Rule E11).

Let us take few examples:

1. Sodium E 111

Analysis

E = Chemistry
1 = substance (Inorganic)
1 = Group 1
1-= Period

2. Calcium E 122

Analysis

E = Chemistry
1 = Substance (Inorganic)
2 = Group 2
2 = Period

3. Sulphur E 161

Analysis

E = Chemistry
1 = Substance (Inorganic)
6 = Group 6
1 = Period

The group of digits following the initial digit '1' may be termed the Element Number.

(Rule E 111)

Eg: Calium 1<u>22</u> Element Number.

Element means substance consisting entirely atoms of the same atomic number.

If a book deals primarily with a hydroxyl or a basic oxide of an Element, its substance of the constituent element i.e the element whose hydroxyl or basic oxide forms the primary subject matter of the book, and the valency member i.e the Arabic numeral representing the valency element in the oxide (Rule E 120). Valency Number means the combining power of an atom, the number of hydrogen atoms which an atom will combine with or replace.

Here are few worked out examples.

Valency of Oxygen in water H2O is 2.

1. Water E2 → Hydrogen or Basic Oxcide
   1 0 → Hydrogen (X10)

2. Sulphuric Acid
   E → Acid
   3 6 1 → Sulphur (X 6 1)

3. Gold Chloride E
   4 → Salt
   18 → Gold (X18)
   71 → Chlorine (71)

4. Sodium Chlorine E4 → Salt
   11 → Sodium (X11)
   71 → Chlorine (71)

5. Sodium Oxide E 4 → Salt
   11 → Sodium (X11)
   60 → Oxygen (60)

6. Nitric Acid E
   3 → Acid
   5 0 → Nitrogen (X50)

7. Potassium Permanganate
   E 4 → Salt
   12 → Potassium (X12)
   72 → Manganese
   60 → Oxygen (X60)

Valency Number according to groups. In general, elements in the same group display similar valency which is numerically equal to the Group Number.

Eg: Synthesis of sulphuric acid

E 3 → Acid
6 1 → Sulphur Valiancy (X61)
: 4 → Synthesis [E] [2P]

8.5.1 Examples

The following are some more worked out examples.

1. Organic analytical chemistry

Analysis

Chemistry = E (MC)
Organic Sub. = 5 [P]
Analysis = :3 [E][2P]

Synthesis

E + 5 + :3 = E5 : 3

2. Physical chemistry of silicates

Analysis

Chemistry = E (MC)
Oxide = 2 [P]
Silicon = 41 (I41)
Oxygen = 60 (I60)
Physical = :2 [E] [2P]

Synthesis

E + 2 + 41 + 60 + :2 = E24160:2

3. Chemical analysis of sulphuric acid

Analysis

Chemistry = E (MC)
Acid = 3[P]
Sulphur = 61 (I61)
Analysis = :3[E][2P]
Chemical = ,J[2P2] for 3 of [E]

Synthesis

E + 3 + 61 + :3 + ,J = E361 : 3,J

4. Chemical analysis food

Analysis

Chemistry = E (MC)
Food = (J3) to be got by (SD)
Analysis = :3 [E] [2P]

Synthesis

E + (J3) + :3 = E (J3) : 3

5. Thermodynamic properties of Nitrogen

Analysis

Chemistry = E (MC)
Oxide = 2[P]
Nitrogen = 50 (I50)
Group No. = 5 → Valency No. Valency No is group No.
Thermodynamics = :24 [E] [2P]

Synthesis

E + 2 + 50 + 5 + :24 = E 2505 : 24

Self Check Exercise – 4

(a) Colorimetric method of analysis
(b) Synthesis of aromatic compound
(c) Molecular structure of Plutonium dioxide
(d) Chemical analysis of milk
(e) Biochemical qualitative analysis of vegetable alkaloid
(f) Annual report of the Director of National Chemical Laboratory, Pune for the year 1998.
(g) India Journal of Biochemistry, 1998
(h) Synthesis of Zinc Sulphide
(i) History of National Metallurgical Laboratory, Jamshadpur.
(j) Comparative study organic and inorganic chemistry

8.5.1 Technology

An Applied Science. Technical method of achieving a practical purpose. The totality of the means employed to provide objects necessary for human sustenance and comfort. The facet formula for F Technology is as follows:

F[E] : [E] [2P]

Where [P] = Substance

[E] [2P] = Problem

8.6.1 Rules

As per F1 (Pl.77) the foci in [P] are same as for E Chemistry and in addition those given in chapter F of schedules (P2.50).

As per rule F22 (P1.77) a book giving an account of some aspects of the problems of Technology in general, the second digit onwards in the subdivisions of the problem division '8 Manipulation' of the (MC) E Chemistry may be used to represent the corresponding problem. As per rule F23 (P1.78) if a book presents process isolates as well as problem isolates the process isolates should be added first and problem isolates there after. The two isolate numbers should be separated by a: Colon

8.6.2 Examples

Here are few worked out examples:

1. Manufacturing of Iron

Analysis

Technology = (MC)

Iron = 182 [P] taken from [P] of E Chemistry

Synthesis

F + 182 = F 182

2. Crystallization of Protein

Analysis

Technology = F(MC)

Protein = 92 [P] taken from [P] of E Chemistry

Crystallization = :31 [E] [2P] as per rule F22

Synthesis

F+ 92Z2 + :31(831) = F92Z2:31

3. Fermentation process of wine

Analysis

Technology = F(MC)

Wine = 547 [P]

Fermentation = :7(8-7) [E] [2P] as per rule F22

Synthesis

F 6+ 547 +:7 = F547 :7

4. Analytical methods in distillation process of beer

Analysis

Technology = F (MC)

Beer = 548 [P]

Distillation = :35(835) [E] [2P]

Analytical method = :3 [E] [2P]

Note As per rule F23, process isolates be added first followed by problem isolate

Synthesis

F + 548 + :35 + :3 = F548:35:3

Self Check Exercise-5

(a) Distillation of Grape wine

(b) Technology of sugar crystallization

(c) Electroplating

(d) Glass blowing technology

(e) Fatigue study of steel alloy

(f) Industrial polarization of methane

(g) Coloring of tanning material

(h) Annual Report of Indian Institute of Technology, Chennai for the year 1998

(i) Functions of Central Food Technology Research Institute, Mysore

(j) Annual report of the Chairman of TISCO, Jamshedpur for the year 1998.

8.7 SUMMARY

In the preceeding of sections we have introduced you to art of classifying documents falling under Mathematical and Physical Sciences. The (MCs) falling under these two partial comprehension's are B Mathematics, C Physics, D Engineering, E Chemistry and F Technology. The (MCs) B Mathematics and C Physics are divided on the lines of canonical divisions. The facet formula of each of these (MCs) are explained and supported by worked out examples. The relevant rules from part 1: Theory has been cited to articulate the intricacies in the construction of class number. The occurrence of each facet in a given title has been analysed citing the relevant focal number and synthesized to arrive at coextensive class number.

Through self check exercises provided for under each (MC), you will have ample opportunity for classifying documents with CC. This practice would keep you in good stead to apply various rules of classification presented in part 1 of CC.

8.8.1 Answer to Self Check Exercises

Exercise-1

(A) B97
(B) B6:23
(C) B38:92
(D) B6M,2
(E) B9m44,N97
(F) B93:57.44'N98
(G) B9.56,f2,G,1'N96
(H) B280fX:8K
(I) B9ur 173
(J) B9430v5:68

Exercise-2

(A) C216
(B) C5:28
(C) CurM79
(D) C41:24
(E) Ce
(F) C56:55

(G) C51:38N28

(H) C9B3:11.44,f3,9N5,1'N98r

(I) C:f3

(J) CN2,5:34

Exercise-3

(A) D4168:4.44185.6G

(B) D5125:85

(C) D7,13:7.4416.NS

(D) D85526.4416.HYD

(E) D66,8(M148)

(F) D3,94.4481.ND'N98'n3

(G) C4:7ObD64,121

(H) D66wM61

(I) D66.4413, k, KSEB1N98r

(J) D660v5

Exercise-4

(A) Exercise:3,E1

(B) E7:4

(C) E269360:218

(D) E0K31:71):3,5

(E) E9G,92J:33

(F) E.44,f39N5,1N98r

(G) E9Gm44,N98

(H) E42361:4

(I) E191.44,f3,9N5v

(J) E10m5

Exercise-5

(A) F547(J374):35

(B) F(J94):31

(C) F191:6

(D) F:96

(E) F1824:94

(F) F611:56

(G) F5897:95

(H) F.44e4,9N5'N98r

(I) F531.44,f,9N5:3

(J) F182.4473,h,TISCO,1'N98r

8.9 ASSIGNMENT

Assign class numbers to the following titles:

1. Dictionary of Physical Sciences
2. The Philosophy of Science
3. Great scientific experiments
4. The foundations of Mathematics
5. Teaching mathematics and its applications
6. Under graduate algebra
7. The state of Art of Numerical Analysis
8. Probability and Random Process
9. A concise dictionary of Astronomy, London 1991
10. The quantum theory of light
11. Introduction to Analytic dynamics
12. Atom nuclei and their particles
13. Studies in History of Chemistry
14. Basic chemical Thermo dynamics
15. Nuclear power Technology
16. Motor Vehicle workshop organization
17. Natural Rubber Science and Technology.
18. The Origins and Early Development of the Heavy Chemical Industry in France
19. Structure of Inorganic Chemistry
20. Carbohydrate Chemistry

UNIT 9

Main Classes under Biological Sciences

9.0 OBJECTIVES

In Unit 8 we have introduced you to the art of classification of titles under Mathematical and Physical Sciences. In this unit we will introduce you to classification of titles under Biological Sciences. After going through this unit you should be able to:

- Grasp the rules of classification pertaining to main classes under Biological Sciences
- Know the facet formula of each of the (MC) and its implications, and
- Assign class numbers to titles falling under the (MCs) G Biology, H Geology, HX Mining, I Botany, J Agriculture, K Zoology, KX animal husbandry and L Medicine.
- Assign class numbers to titles falling under the (MCs) G Biology, H Geology, HX Mining, I Botany, J Agriculture, K Zoology, KX Animal Husbandry and L Medicine.

9.1 INTRODUCTION

In unit 8 we have introduced you to classify documents under Mathematical and Physical Science. In this unit we will introduce you to classify documents under Biological Sciences. The (MCs) falling under Biological Sciences are: G Biology, H Geology, HX

Mining, I Botany, J Agriculture, K Zoology, KX Animal

Husbandry and L Medicine. Please refer to chapter 1 (P2.4) of the schedules for list of (MCs). Each (MC) will be introduced to you citing its facet formula and relevant and important rules stated in part 1 of CC and will be demonstrated by worked out examples. Let us take up each one of these (MCs) under Biological Sciences.

9.2 G BIOLOGY

"A Branch of knowledge that deals with living organisms and vital processes.'' The facet formula for G Biology is as follows:

G [P] :[E] [2P]

Where Foci in [P] = Organ and Special Grouping

Foci in [E] [2P] = Problem

9.2.1 Rules

A general account of life as biological phenomena should be given the Organ Number 1. As per rule G233 (P1.79) when the focus in the Problem Facet is 33 Metabolism or 341 or 345 or 346 or any of their subdivisions [2M] should be added. It may be called Substance Facet. The foci in it are the same as for [P] of E Chemistry. As per rule G25 (P1.79) when the focus in [E] is 12 to 18 or 5 or any of its subdivisions [S] may have to be added.

9.2.2 Worked out Examples

The following are some worked out examples:

1. Marin Biology

   Analysis

   Biology = G (MC)

   Marine = 9555 [P]

   Synthesis

   G + 9555 = G 9555

2. Wood Land ecology of India

   Analysis

   Biology = G(MC)

   Forest = 95124 [P]

   Ecology = :[E] [2P]

India = .44 as per rule G25, we have to add [S]

Synthesis

G + 95124 + ;5 + .44 = G95124:5.44

3. Flora and Fauna of China

Analysis

Biology = G (MC)

Flora and Fauna = :12 [E] [2P]
(Natural History)

China = .41 [S]

Synthesis

G + :12 + .41 = G:12.41

4. Study of fasting on the intestinal absorption of Carbohydrates.

Analysis

Biology = G (MC)

Intestine = 25 [P] to be taken from [P] of L Medicine

Fasting = :346 [E] [2P]

NOTE: As per rule G233, [2M] should be taken from [P] of E Chemistry, Carbohydrates = ;68 [2M] from [P] of E Chemistry

Synthesis

G + 25 + ;346 + ; 68 = G25:346;68

5. Proceedings of the International Conference on the Origin of life on earth held at London, 19-24 august, 1998.

Analysis

Biology = G (MC)

Evolution = :66 [E] 1
(Origin of life}

Conference = p (ACI = Applicable before Space Facet)

International = .1 [S]

1998 = ,N98 [T] = Both appear as Fundamental Category Personality

Synthesis

C + :66 + p + 1 + ,N98 = G:66pl, N98

6. Physiology of Cell

Analysis

Biology = G (MC)

Cell = 11 [P]

Physiology = :3 [E] [2P]

Synthesis

G + 11 + :3 = G11:3

7. Structure genes in adolescent

Analysis

Adolescent = G9D (Special)

Gene = 116[P]

Structure = :2 [E] [2P]

NOTE: When ever we add focus from [P] facet to a system or special it should proceeded by, Comma.

Synthesis

G9D + ,116 + :2 = G9D, 116:2

8. Microphotography of Nucleoli

Analysis

Biology = G (MC)

Nucleoli = 1135 [P]

Microphotography = :1995 [E][2P]

Synthesis

G + 1135 + :1995 = G1135:1995

Self Check Exercise –1

(a) The Structure of Cell

(b) Ecology of North American deserts

(c) Charles Darwin (1809-1882): The Descent of Man

(d) Introduction to Biotechnology

(e) Biological Nomenclature Today

(f) The Oxford dictionary of Natural History, 1993

(g) The Biology and Chemistry of Polymers

(h) Introduction to Biophysics

(i) Evolutionary biology of aging

(j) Molecular Biology

9.3 H GEOLOGY

"A Science that deals with the history of the earth and its life especially as recorded in rocks.'' It is further divided on canonical lines such as:

H1 Mineralogy
H2 Petrology
H3 Structural Geology
H5 Stratigraphy
H6 Paleontology
H7 Economic Geology
H8 Cosmic Hypothesis

For some of the canonical divisions we find facet formula and their implications are explained in the theory part (P1.80). The following are few worked out examples for some of the important Canonical divisions.

9.3.1 H1 Minerology

The facet formula for H1 Mineralogy is as follows:

H1 [P] : [E] [2P]

Where foci in [P] = Substance (Same as for E Chemistry)

Foci in [E] [2P] = Problem

1. Prospecting of precious stones

Analysis

Mineralogy = H1 (CNC)
Precious Stones = 9 [P]
Prospecting = :15 [E] [2P]

Synthesis

H1 + 15 + :864 = H19:15

2. Artificial Production of Pearls

Analysis

Minierlogy = H1(CNC)

Pearl = 98[8]

Artificial Production = :164[E][2P]

Synthesis

H1 + 98 + :164 = H 198 : 164

3. Occurrence of Zinc

Analysis

Mineralogy = H1 (CNC)

Zinc = 123 [P] To be taken from [P] of E Chemistry

Occurrence = :155 [E] [2P]

Synthesis

H1 + 123 + :155 = H1123:155

9.3.2 H2 Petrology

The facet formula for H2 Petrology is as follows:

H2[P] :[E] [2P]

Where foci in [P] = Substance

Foci in [E] Analysis = Problem. Same as those for H1 Mineralogy

1. Classification of Plutonic Rocks

Analysis

Petrology = H2 (CNC)

Plutonic Rock = 17 [P]

Classification = :8115 [E] [2P]

Synthesis

H2 + 17 + :8115 = H217:8115

2. Genesis of Igneous Rocks

Analysis

Petrology = H2 (CNC)

Igneous Rocks = 1 [P]

Genesis = :16 [E] [2P]

Synthesis

H2 + 1 + :16 = H21:16

3. Prospecting of Bog iron ore

Analysis

Petrology = H2 (CNC)

Bog iron Ore = 34823 [P]

Prospecting = :15 [E] [2P]

Synthesis

H2 + 34823 + :15 = H234823:15

9.3.3 H7 Economic Geology

The facet formula for H7 is as follows:

H7 [P] : [E] [2P]

Where foci in [P] = Substance, Same as for E Chemistry

Foci in [E] Analysis = Problem same as for H1 Mineralogy

1. Mineral resources of South Africa

Analysis

Economic Geology = H7 (CNC)

South Africa = .63 [S]

Synthesis

H7 + .63 = H7.63

2. Prospecting of copper deposits in Andhra Pradesh

Analysis

Economic Geology = H7 (CNC)

Copper = 113 [P] To be taken from E Chemistry

Prospecting = :15 [E] To be taken from H1 Mineralogy

Andhra Pradesh = .4416 [S]

Synthesis

H7 + 113 + :15 + .4416 + H7113:15.4416

3. Investigation of Occurrence of manganese deposits in Germany during Second World War (1938-1945)

Analysis

Economic Geology = H7 (CNC)

Manganese = 172 [P]

Occurrence = :155 [E] [2P]

Germany = .55 [S]

Second World War (1938-1945) = 'N38→'N45 [T]

Investigation = :f(PCI) [E]

Synthesis

H7 + 172 +:155 +.55 + 'N38 → 'N45 +: f = H7172:155.55'N38 → 'N45:f

9.3.4 Other Canonical Divisions

The following are some more worked out examples covering other Canonical Divisions

1. Report of the Commission on Chamoli Earthquake

Analysis

Dynamic Geology = H4 (CNC)

Earthquake = 132 (Further division of H4)

Chamoli (UP) = .4452.CH [S]

1999 = 'N99 [T]

Commission Report = t (ACI – Applicable after Time Facet)

Synthesis

H4 + 132 + .4452.CH + 'N99+t = H4132.4452.CH'N99t

2. Triassic fishes of New South Wales

Analysis

Paleontology = H6 (CNC)

Fish = 92 [P] Taken from [P] of K Zoology

New South Wales = .82 [S]

Trissic period = 'A3<u>1</u> (i.e. H53<u>1</u>)

Synthesis

H6 + 92 + .82 + 1A31 = H692.82'A31

3. Cretaceous Stratigraphy of Iceland

Analysis

Stratigraphy = H5 (CNC)

Cretaceous = 34 (Division of H5)

Iceland = .574 [S]

Synthesis

H55 + 34 + .574 = H534.574

9.4 HX MINING

The process or business of working mines.

The facet formula for HZ Mining is as follows:

HX[P], [P2] : [E] [2P]

Where foci in [P] = Substance. To be got from [P] of E chemistry and F Technology

Foci in [P2] = Work

Foci in [E] [2P] = Problem

The following are few worked out examples.

1. Coal Mining

Analysis

Mining = HX (MC)

Coal = 551[P] Taken from [P] of F Technology

Synthesis

HX + 551 = HX551

2. Underground roads in Copper Mines

Analysis

Mining = HX (MC)

Copper = 113 [P] Taken from [P] of E Chemistry
Underground roads = ,4[P2]

Synthesis

HX + 113 +,4 = HX113,4

3. Prevention of accidents in Gold Mines

Analysis

Mining = HX (MC)
Gold = 118 [P] Taken from [P] of E Chemistry
Accident = :4 [E] [2P]
Prevention = :5 (Seminal Mnemonic, See page 1.32 of CC)

Synthesis

HX + 118 + :4 + :5 = HX118:4:5

4. BSI glossary of mining terms in English

Analysis

Mining = HX (MC)
English Language = :(P111): Please refer rule P48 at Page 1.106

Synthesis

HC + :(P111) = HX: (P111)

5. Annual report of the Director of Central Mining Research Institute, Dhanbad for 1998

Analysis

Mining = HX (MC)
India = .44[S]
Research body = ,f (PCI – Personality Isolate),
Research Institute = CMRI (Alphabetical Device)
Director = ,1 (Taken from [P2] of V History)
1998 = 'N98 [T]
Annual report = r (ACI-Application only after Space Facet)

Synthesis

HX + .44 + ,f + CMRI + ,1 + 'N98 + r = HX.44,f, CMRI,1'N98r

Self Check Execise-2

(a) The story of gems

(b) Genesis of ruby

(c) Artificial Production of Topaz

(d) Classification Volcanic rocks

(e) Vertebrate fossils of Alaska

(f) Triassic fishes of New South Wales

(g) Paleozoic stratigraphy of Greenland

(h) Annual report of the Director General of Geological Survey of India for the year 1998

(i) Annual report of the Director of National Geophysical Research Institute (NGRI) (Estd. 1961) Hyderabad for 1998

(j) Blasting in Coal Mines

(k) Drainage problems in Mining

(l) Thermodynamics for Geologists

(m) Theoretical Geochemistry

(n) Minerals and Mining in Antarctica

(o) Annual report of the Chairman of Singareni Collaries A.P. for the year 1998.

9.5 I BOTANY

"A branch of Biology dealing with plant life." The facet formula for I Botany is as follows:

I [P], [P2] : [E] [2P]

Analysis

Where foci in [P] = Natural Group

Foci in [P2] = organ

Foci in [E] [2P] = Problem. Same as in G Biology

The following are few worked out examples

1. New concepts in flowering plants

Analysis

Botany = I (MC)

Floweirng Plant = 5[P]

Synthesis

I + 5 = 15

2. Plant diseases

Analysis

Botany = I (MC)

Disease = :4 [E] Taken from [E] of G Bilogy

Synthesis

I + :4 = I:4

3. Control of diseases of Leaves of rose plants

Analysis

Botany = I (MC)

Rose Plant = 831 [P]

Leaf = ,15 [P2]

Diseases = :4[E] Taken from [E] of G Bilogy

Control = :5 [2E] Taken from [2E] of G Biology

Synthesis

I + 831 + ,15 +:4 + :5 = I831,15:4:5

4. Photosynthesis

Analysis

Botany = I (MC)

Metabolism = :33 [E] Taken from [E] of G Biology

Starch = ;6892 [M] Taken from [P] of E Chemistry

NOTE: As per rule G233 (P1.79) problem focus 33 is to be augmented with [2M]. The focus is to be taken from [P] of E Chemistry

Synthesis

I + :33 + ;6892 = I:33;6892

5. The structure of seeds

Analysis

Botany = I (MC)

Seed = ,178 [P2]

Structure = :2 [E] Taken from [E] of G Biology

Synthesis

I + ,178 + :2 = I,178:2

6. Paleobotany

Analysis

Botany = I (MC)

Paleobotany = :8 [E]

Synthesis

I + :8 = I : 8

7. Bacterial plant diseases

Analysis

Botany = I (MC)

Bacterial diseases = :424 [E] Taken from [E] of G Biology

Synthesis

I + :424 = I:424

8. Bulletin of Botanical Survey of India, Calcutta, 1998

Analysis

Botany = I (MC)

Bulletin = m (Periodical) (ACI- Appicable only be fore space facet)

India = 44 [P]

1998 = ,N98 [P2]

Synthesis

I + m + 44 + ,N98 = Im44,N98

9. Anatomy of Dicotyledons

Analysis

Botany = I(MC)]

Dicotyledon = 8 [P]

Anatomy = :2 [E] Taken from [E] of G Biology

Synthesis

I + 8 + :2 = I8:2

10. Annual report of the Director of Botanical Survey of India for the year, 1998

Botany = I (MC)

India = .44 [S]

Investigating body = ,f (PCI-Personality CI)

Botanical Survey of India = ,9N5 (See rule 271 at page 20 of Annexure)

Director = ,1 [P] Taken from [P2] of V History

Annual Report = r (ACI-Appliable after Space Facet)

1998 = 'N98

Synthesis

I + .44 + ,f + ,9N5 + , 1 + r + 'N98 = I.44, f, 9N5, 1rN98

9.6 J AGRICULTURE

"The science or art of cultivating the soil, producing crops and raising live stock," The facet formula for J Agriculture is as follows:

J [P], [P2] :[E] [2P] : [2E] [3P]

Where foci in [P] = Plant (to be got by combination of Utility Array and Part Array of [P]

[P2] = Organ (Same as of Part Array)

[E] [2P] = Problem

[2E] [3P] = Operation

9.6.1 Rules

The first significant digit of Plan Number is Utility Number.

The second is Part Number. The third either Genus or species to which the Plant belongs.

If the third significant digit reprsetns Genus, the fourth represetns species.

Eg: Rice Plant J381 → Genus (Favoured Category Device)

Genus and Species are enumerated udner Favoured Cateogry Principle and Alphabetical Device

Eg: Pine Apple J3752

The foci in [P] in j Agriculture is derived by the combination of Utility Array and part Array. The foci for these two arrays are listed at the beginnng of schedule for J Agriculture (P2.64)

Examples: 1. Fruits for Eating J37
2. Fruits for Oil J57
3. Seeds for Food J38
4. Seeds for Oil J58
6. Stimulant leaves J45

And so on

Specific cultivar variety is to be got by alphabetical Device (AD)

Examples: Sona Masuri Rice J381 SM (got by (AD))
Bansi Wheat J382 B (got by (AD))

9.6.2 Worked out Examples

The following are few worked out examples

1. Physiology of rice plant

Analysis

Agriculture = J (MC)
Rice = 381 [P]
Physiology = :93 [E]

Synthesis

J + 381 +:93 = J381 : 93

2. Mango leaf disease

Analysis

Agriculture = J (MC)

Mango = 3751 [P]

Leaf = ,5 [P2] Taken from Part Array

Disease = :4 [E]

Synthesis

J +2751 + ,5 +:4 = J3751,5:4

3. Cold Storage of Potatoes

Analysis

Agriculture = J (MC)

Potato = 374 [P]

Harvesting = :7 [E]

Cold Storage = :84 [2E] [3P] for 7 of [E]

NOTE: Without using [E] we cannot proceed to [2E]

Synthesis

J + 374 +:7 + :84 = J374:7:84

4. Composting green manure

Analysis

Agriculture = J (MC)

Manure = :2 [E]

Green = 1 [2P] for 2 manure of [E]

Composting = :6 [2E] for 2 manure of [E]

Synthesis

J + :2 + 1 + :6 = J:21:6

5. Control measures for bacterial diseases in the flowers of Coconut

Analysis

Agriculture = J(MC)

Coconut = 582 [P]

Flower = ,6 [P2] Taken from Part Array

Disease = :4 [E]

Bacteria = 24 [2P] Taken from foci in 2P for 4 of [E] of L Medicine

Control measure = :55 [2E] Taken from foci in [2E] [3P] of L Medicine

Synthesis

J + 582 +, 6 + :4 + 24 + :55 = J582,6:424:55

6. Hand book of Indian forest statistics, 1998

Analysis

Forestry = JB (System)

India = .44 [S]

Statistics = s (ACI-Applicable after Space Facet)

1998 = N98

Analysis

JB +.44 + s + N98 = JB.44sN98

7. Report of the committee on Seed Multiplication Schemes, Maharashtra, 1998

Analysis

Agriculture = J (MC)

Seed = 38 [P]

Multiplication (Breedings) = :6 [E]

Maharastra = .4435 [S]

1998 = 'N98 [T]

Committee report = t (ACI-Applicable only after Time Facet)

Synthesis

J + 38 +:6 + .4435 +'N98 + t = J38:6.4435'N988t

8. Annual report of the Director of Indian Agricultural Research Institute (IARI) New Delhi for the year 1998.

Analysis

Agriculture = J (MC)

India = .44 [S]

Research Institute	=	,f (PCI – Personality (CI))
IARI	=	,9N4 (By (CD) – See rule 1.48 at page 20 of the annexure
Director	=	,1 Taken from [P2] of V History
Report	=	r (ACI – Applicable only after Space Facet)
1998	=	N98 [T]

Synthesis

J + .44 + , f + 9N4 + ,1 + r + N98 = J.44,f,9N4, 1rN98

Self Check Exercise –3

(a) Research on Plant Physiology

(b) Structure of Seeds

(c) Concise Oxford Dictionary of Botany, 1992

(d) Botany for Degree Student

(e) Journal of Experimental Botany, London, 1950

(f) Nitrogen metabolism of Plants

(g) Plant geography of India

(h) Anatomy of Monocotyledons

(i) Agricultural marketing

(j) Dry land forming, a systematic approach

(k) The Chemistry of Soils

(l) Annual report of the Director of Central Banana Research Station, Aduthurai (Tamilnadu) (Estd. 1949) for the year 1998.

9.7 K ZOOLOGY

"A Science that deals with animals and is the branch of biology concerned with animal kingdom and its members as individuals and classes and with animal life.''. The facet formula for K Zoology is as follows:

K[P]:[E][2P]

Where foci in [P] = Natural Group

Foci in [E] [2P] = Problem (To be got from [E] [2P] of G biology

The following are few worked out examples:

1. Pathology of Birds

Analysis

Zoology = K(MC)

Birds = 96 [P]

Pathology = :4 [E] Taken from [E] of G Biology

Synthesis

K + 96 + :4 = K96:4

2. Social Life of animals

Analysis

Zoology = K (MC)

Social Life = :56 [E] Taken from [E] of G Biology

Synthesis

K + :56 = K:56

3. Wild animals of India

Analysis

Zoology = K (MC)

Wild Animal = 9954 [P]

India = .44 [S]

Synthesis

K + 9954 + .44 = K9954.44

4. Fresh Water fish of East Africa

Analysis

Zoology = K (MC)

Fish (Pices) = 92 [P]

East Africa = .69B (9B) [S]

Synthesis

K + 92 + .69B = K 92. 69B

5. Methods of Mammalian Reproduction

Analysis

Zoology = K (MC)

Mammals = 97 [P]

Reproduction = :67 [E] Taken for foci in [E] of G Biology

Synthesis

K + 97 + :67 = K97:67

6. Annual report of the Director General of Zoological Survey of India (1950) for the year 1998

Analysis

Zoology = K (MC)

India = .44[S]

Investigating body = ,f (PCI-Personality) (CI))

Zoological Survey of India = .9N5 (By CD) se rule 1.48 at page 20 of the annexure)

Director General = ,1 Taken from [P2] of V History

Report = r (ACI-Applicable only after Space Facet)

1998 = N98[T]

Synthesis

K + .44 + ,f + 9N5 + ,1 + r + N98 = K.44,f,9N5, 1rN98

9.8 KX ANIMAL HUSBANDRY

"A branch of agriculture concerned with production and care of domestic animals'' The facet formula for KX Animal Husbandry as follows:

KX [P]: [E] [2P] : [2E] [3P]

Where foci in [P] = Animal

Foci in [E] [2P] = Problem

Foci in [2E][3P] = Operation

Like J Agriculture foci in [P] is based on the combination of Utility Array and Part Array. The foci for these two arrays is provided at the beginning of the schedule for KX Animal Husbandry (P.2.79). The following are few worked out examples.

1. Poultry farming

   Analysis

   Animal Husbandry = KX (MC)

   Poultry = 351 [P]

   Synthesis

   KX + 351 = KX351

2. Cold Storage of Milk

   Analysis

   Animals Husbandry = KX (MC)

   Secretion = 31 [P]

   Produce = :7 [E]

   Milk = 1 [2P] for [E]

   Cold Storage = :84 [2E] [3P] As in J Agriculture

   Analysis

   KX + 31 + : 7 + 1 : 84 = KX31:71:84

3. Treatment of diseases of a farm animals

   Analysis

   Animal Husbandry = KX (MC)

   Diseases = :4[E]

   Treatment = :6 [2E] As in L Medicine

   Synthesis

   KX + :4 + :6 = KX:4:6

4. Pet dogs, their management and training

   Analysis

   Animal Husbandry = KX (MC)

   Dog = 541 [P]

   Training = :8 [E]

Synthesis

KX + 541 + :8 = KX541:8

5. An anatomical atlas of ox

Analysis

Animal Husbandry	= KX (MC)
Bull (Ox)	= 441 [P]
Anatomy	= :2 [E]
Atlas	= f (ACI-Applicable only before Space Facet)

Synthesis

KX + 441 + :2 + f = KX441:2f

6. Annual report of Director of Central Dairy Research Institute, Karnal for the year 1998

Analysis

Animal Husbandry	= KC (MC)
Secretion	= 31 [P]
Produce	= :7 [E]
Milk	= 1[2P] for [E]
India	= .44 [S]
Research Institute	= ,f[PCI-Personality (CI)]
CDR Institute	= ,9N6 (CD) (see rule 1.48 at page 20 in the annexure)
Director	= ,1 [P2] Taken from [P2] of V History
Report	= r (ACI-Applicable only after Space Facet)
1998	= N98 [T]

Synthesis

KX+31+:7+1+.44+,f+9N6,1+r+'N98 = KX31:7.44,f,9N6, 1rN98

Self Check Exercise-4

(a) Introduction to Vertebrate Zoology

(b) Elephants, a short account of their natural history

(c) The Oxford Dictionary of Zoology, 1991

(d) Foundation of Animal Development

(e) The biology of millipedes

(f) Crocodile breeding in River Krishna

(g) Biography Salim Ali (1897-1987)

(h) The ecology of Wood Land Rodents

(i) Protein metabolism in farm animals

(j) Sheep production in the Tropics

(k) Concise Veterinary dictionary, London 1998

(l) Veterinary Genetics

(m) Anatomy of domestic animals

(n) Introduction to Sericulture

(o) Foot rot in Cows

(p) Treatment of T.B. in Cattle

9.9 L MEDICINE

"The science and art of preventing, alleviating or curing disease esp, the branch of this field concerned with the non-surgical treatment of disease." The facet formula for L Medicine as follows:

L[P]:[E][2P]:[2E][3P]

Where foci in [P] = Organ

Foci in [E] [2P] = Problem

Foci in [2E] [3P] = Handling for 4 Diseases of [E]

9.91 Rules

The digit 1 and its subdivisions under [P] represent regional divisions. The digits 2-8 represent functional divisions. As per rule L113 (P1.88) parts of functional organs within a regional organ may be indicated by adding to the regional organ number by super Imposition Device (SID), the appropriate functional focus being used as Super Imposed focus.

Examples:

1. Arteries of thorax L15-37

2. Skin of Face L181-87
3. Nerve Cells L11-74

As per rule L91(P1.89) if an organ number is attached to a "Special Number'' or "System Number'' it should be preceded by a, comma. If a 'Special Number' is attached to a 'System Number' the former should be preceded by a, comma

Examples:

1. Treatment of Tetanus by Ayurveda LB 72:4241:6
2. Typhoid in Children L9, 24:4241
4. Treatment of Typhoid in Children by Homeopathy LL, 9, 24:4241:6

9.9.2 Worked out Examples

The following are some of the worked out examples:

1. Human Blood

Analysis

Medicine = L (MC)

Blood = 35 [P]

Synthesis

L + 35 = L 35

2. Lung Diseases

Analysis

Medicine = L (MC)

Lung = 45 [P]

Disease = 4[E]

Synthesis

L + 45 + :4 = L45:4

3. Treatment of T.B of lungs

Analysis

Medicine = L(MC)

Lungs = 45 [P]

Disease = :4 [E]

Tuberculosis = 21 [2P] for 4 of [E]

Treatment = :6[2E] [3P]

Synthesis

L + 45 + :4 + 21 + :6 = L45:421:6

4. X-ray diagnosis of Epilepsy

Analysis

Medicine = L (MC)

Central Nervous System = 71 [P]

Disease = :4 [E]

Complicated functioning = 53 [2P] for 4 of [E]

X-ray diagnosis = :3253 [2E] [3P]

Synthesis

L + 71 + :4 + 53 + :3253 = L71:453:3253

5. Manual of Surgery

Analysis

Medicine = L(MC)

Disease = :4 [E]

Surgery = :7 [2E] [3P]

NOTE: Without first using [E] we cannot directly use [2E] [3P]. The use of [2E] [3P] is dependent upon use of [E] [2P]. There is no Specific (CI) Number for 'Manual' in CC.

Synthesis

L + :4+ :7 = L:4:7

6. Ayurvedic Treatment of Paralysis

Analysis

Medicine = L (MC)

Ayurveda = LB (System)

Sensory nerve = ,76 [P]

Disease = :4[E]

Atrophy = 11 [2P] for 4 of [E]

Treatment = :6 [2E] [3P]

Synthesis

LB +,76 + :4 + 11 + :6 = LB, 76:411:6

7. Case studies in birth control

Analysis

Female Medicine = L9F (Special)

Birth Control = :394 [E]

Case study = y7 (ACI-Applicable only before Space Facet)

Synthesis

L9F +:394 + y7 = L9F: 394y7

8. Psychotherapy of Neurology

Analysis

Medicine = L (MC)

Nervous System = 7[P]

Disease = :4[E]

Psychotherapy = :691[2E][3P]

Synthesis

L + 7 + :4 + :691 = L7:4:691

9. Handbook of Dermatology

Analysis

Medicine = L (MC)

Skin = 87 [P]

Disease = :4 [E]

Treatment = :6[2E] [3P]

Synthesis

L + 87 + :4 + :6 = L87:4:6

10. Treatment of Skin Diseases of Children by Unani system of Medicine

Analysis

Unani = LD (System)

Child (Medicine) = L9C (Special)

Skin = ,87 [P]

Disease = :4 [E]

Treatment :6[2E][3P]

Note: As per rule L91 (P1.89) if a 'Special Number' is added to a 'System Number' the former should be proceeded by, comma. If an Organ Number is added to 'Special Number' or 'System Number' it should be proceeded by a, Comma.

Synthesis

LD + ,L9C + ,87 + :4 + :6 = LD,9C,87:4:6

Self Check Exercise-5

(a) Tuberculosis of Lungs

(b) Asthama

(c) Biography of Florence Nightingale (1820)

(d) Out line of Orthopedic Surgery

(e) Pediatric Neuro-surgery

(f) Annual report of the Director of Public Health, Government of Andhra Pradesh for the year 1998

(g) Siddha cure of dysentery of Old age people

(h) Prevention of dental diseases

(i) American journal of preventive Medicine, 1985

(j) Chemotherapy of infection

(k) Colour atlas of Cardio Vascular Pathology

(l) Histopathology of Liver

9.10 SUMMARY

In the proceeding sections we have introduced you to art and technique of classifying titles under Biological Sciences. The (MCs) falling under this Partial Comprehension are: G biology, H Geology, HX Mining, I Botany, J Agriculture, K Zoology, KX Animal Husbandry and L Medicine. The facet formula of each of the (MCs) are explained and supported by worked out examples. The relevant rules form part 1 of CC have been cited to articulate the intricacies in the construction of Class number or Number Building. The occurrence of each facet in a given title has been analysed citing the relevant focal number and synthesized to arrive at Coextensive Class Number. Through self-check exercises provided for under each (MC) you will have ample opportunity for classifying documents with CC. This practice would keep you in good stead to apply various rules of classification presented in Part I of CC.

9.10 ANSWERS TO SELF-CHECK EXERCISES

Exercises-1

(a) G11:2
(b) G955121:5.71
(c) G:66xM09,1
(d) G:(F)
(e) G:11
(f) G:12k56,N96
(g) G0aE1
(h) G(C)
(i) G9E:66
(j) G (C9B1) or C9B1 (G)

Exercise-2

(a) H19v
(b) H1921:16
(c) H195:164
(d) H211:8115
(e) H69.76
(f) H692.82'A31
(g) H51.7191
(h) H.44,f,(M5,1rN98)
(i) H: (C).44,f,9N6,1rN98
(j) HX551:13
(k) HX:52
(l) C4:70bH
(m) H:(E)
(n) H10aH4,983

(o) HX551.4416,k,SC.1rN98

Exercise-3

(a) I:3:f

(b) I,178:2

(c) Ik56,N92

(d) I0bT4

(e) I:fm56,N56,N50

(f) I:33;150

(g) I:(V).44

(h) I7:2

(i) J:(X:51)

(j) J9D

(k) J:1(E)

(l) J3731.44,f,9N49,1rN98

Exercise-4

(a) K9

(b) K9786:2

(c) Kk56,M91

(d) K:7

(e) K412:(G)

(f) K946:(KZ:6).441.plK

(g) K96urM97

(h) K9793:5f

(i) KX:33;92z2

(j) KX783:6.192

(k) KXk56,N98

(l) KX:6

(m) KX:2

(n) KX711:6

(o) KX311,132:4

(p) KX2:421:6

Exercise-5

(a) L45:421

(b) L44:453
(c) L:4wM20
(d) L82:4:7
(e) L9c,7:4
(f) L:5.4416,w,DPH,1rN98
(g) LC,9E,25:474:6
(h) L214:4:5
(i) L:4:5m73,N85
(j) L:42:6:(E)
(k) L32:4:4f
(l) L291:4:4

9.11 ASSIGNMENT

Assign Class Numbers to the following titles

1. Biological Nomenclature Today
2. Horizons of Bio Chemical Engineering
3. Comparative Methods in Evolutionary Biology
4. The Concise Oxford Dictionary of Earth Sciences, 1991
5. Basic Analytical Petrology
6. Tectonic Evolution of North Sea
7. Mine Environment and Ventilation
8. Molecular Plant Pathology
9. Plant Reproductive Ecology
10. A Field guide to the Acacias of Kenya
11. The surface chemistry of soils
12. Plant Disease Management
13. Plantation Forestry in the Tropics
14. The Pasteral Industries in Australia
15. Veterinary Genetics
16. Bio Chemsitry and Physilogy of the Skin
17. The Diagnosis of Congenitial Heart Diseases
18. Kidney Disease
19. A Manual of Practical Vertebrate Morphology
20. The Book of Indian Brids.

UNIT 10

Main Classes Under Humanities

10.0 OBJECTIVES

In unit 9, we have introduced you to the art of classifications of titles under Biological Sciences. In this unit we will introduced you to classification of titles under Humanities. After going through this unit you should be able to:

- Understand the rules of classification pertaining to Main Classes under Humanities.
- Know the facet formula of each of the (MC) and its implications; and
- Assign Class Number to titles falling under the (MCs) N fine Arts, O Literature, P Linguistics, Q Religion and R Philosophy.

10.1 INTRODUCTION

In unit 9 we have introduced you to classify documents under Biological Sciences. In this unit we will introduce you to classify documents under Humanities. The (MCs) which broadly come under Humanities are: N Fine Arts, O Literature, P Linguistics, Q Religion and R Philosophy. Please refer to chapter 1 (P2.4) of the schedules for list of (MCs). Each main class will be introduced to you citing its facet formula and relevant and important rules stated in Part 1 of CC and will be demonstrated by worked out examples.

Let us take up each one of the (MCs) under Humanities.

10.2 N FINE ARTS

"Arts as Painting, Sculpture, Music concerned primarily with creation of beautiful objects''. It is further divided on Canonical lines such as:

NA Architecture

NB Town Planning

ND Sculpture

NM Graphic Arts

NQ Painting

NR Music

NT Theatre

For some of the important and prominent Canonical Classes (CNC) we find facet formula. The (CNC) of the (MC) N Fine Arts will admit of being divided by style. Style is individualized by the Country and the Century of its origin. Style is the manifestation of Personality Facet at two levels i.e. region and epoch. The following table may be applied to any (CNC) of the (MC) N Fine Arts.

Facet	Terms	(IN) by
[P]	Region	(GD)
[P2]	Epoch	(CD)
[P] [P2]	Style	

Style is divided on the basis Region and Epoch, which are to be got by Geographical and Chronological Devices respectively. For almost all Canonical Classes (CNC) of the (MC) N Fine arts Style is Common. The foci listed under [P], [P2] for NA Architecture may be used for other Fine Arts also. For detailed explanation please refer CC Pl.95

10.2.1 NA Architecture

The facet formula for NA Architecture is as follows:

NA[P],[P2][P3],[P4][E]

Where foci in [P] [P2] = style

[P3] = Utility

[P4] = Part

[E][2P] = Technique

Let us take up few worked out examples

1. Indian Architecture

Analysis

Architecture = NA (CNC)

India = 44 [P] to be got by (CD)

Synthesis

NA + 44 = NA 44

2. Mogul Architecture

Analysis

Architecture = NA (CNC)

India = 44[P] to be got by (CD)

Mogal (Period) (16th century) = ,J[P2] to be got by (CD)

Synthesis

NA + 44 + ,J = NA44,J

3. Design of French Museums

Analysis

Architecture = NA (CNC)

France = 53 [P] to be got by (GD)

Museums = ,6[P3]

Design = :3[E]

Synthesis

NA + 53 + ,6 + :3 = NA53,6:3

4. Models of Indian University Library buildings

Analysis

Architecture = NA (CNC0

India = 44 [P] to be got (GD)

Library buildings = 22 [P3]

NOTE: 22 is to be further divided as the [P] of 2 Library science. University Library = 34 (taken from [P] of 2, Library Science)

Model = :8[E]

Synthesis

NA + 44 + ,22 + 34 + :8 = NA44,2234:8

5. Decoration of City dwellings in Tropics

Analysis

Architecture = NA (CNC0

City dwelling = ,35 [P3]

Decoration = ,99 [P4]

Tropics = .192[S]

Analysis

NA + ,35 + ,99 + ,192 = NA,35,99.192

6. Architecture of Music Halls

Analysis

Architecture = NA (CNC)

Other buildings = ,8(A) to be divided by (SD)

Music = NR

Music Halls = , 8(NR) (Subject Device)

Synthesis

NA + ,8(NR) = NA,8(NR)

7. Biography Charles Correa (1930)

Analysis

Architecture = NA (MC)

India = 44[P] to be got by (GD)

Biography = w(ACI- Applicable before Space Facet)

Year of birth (1930) = N3O[P] to be got by (CD)

Synthesis

NA + 44 w + N30 = NA44wN30

10.2.2 NB Town Planning

The facet formula for NB Town Planning is as follows:

NB[P],[P2] [P3],[P4]:[E]

Where foci in [P]	= Region	= To be got by (GD)	Style
Foci in [P2]	= Epoch	= To be got by (CD)	
Foci in [P3]	= Utility		
Foci in [P4]	= Part		
Foci in [E]	= Technique, as for NA Architecture		

The following are some worked out examples

1. Indian Town Planning

Analysis

Town Planning = NB (CNC)

India = 44 [P] to be got by (GD)

Synthesis

NB + 44 = NB44

2. City Planning

Analysis

Town Planning = NB (CNC)

City = ,5[P3]

Synthesis

NB + ,5 = NB,5

3. Models of Parks in towns

Analysis

Town Planning = NB (CNC)

Town = ,3[P3]

Parks = ,66 [P4]

Model = :8[E]

Synthesis

NB + ,3 + ,66 + :8 = NB,3,6:8

4. Elevation of theatres in ancient Roman Cities

Analysis

Town Planning = NB (CNC)

Italy = 52 [P] to be got by (GD)

10th Century = ,D[P2] to be got by (CD)

City = 5 [P3]

Theatre = ,691 [P4]

Elevation = :4[E] to be taken from NA Architecture

Synthesis

NB + 52 + ,D + ,5 + ,691 + :4 NB52,D5,691:4

5. The laws of Indian town parks and recreation grounds

Analysis

Town Planning = NB (CNC)

Town = ,3[P3]

Parks = ,66[P4]

Law = (Z) to be got by (SD)

Synthesis

NB + ,3 + ,66 + (Z) = NB, 3, 66(Z)

10.2.3 ND Sculpture

The facet formula for ND Sculpture is as follows:

ND [P], [P2],[P3],[M]:[E][2P]

Where foci in [P] = Region To be got by (GD) ⎤ Style

Where foci in [P2] = Epoch To be got by (CD) ⎦

Where foci in [P3] = Figure

Where foci in [M] = Material

Where foci in [E] [2P] = Technique

The following are some worked out examples

1. Buddhist Sculpture of human figure

Analysis

Sculpture = ND (CNC)

India = 44 [P] To be got by)GD)/

Buddhist = ,C[P2] to be got by (CD)

Human figure = 1 [P3]

Synthesis

ND + 44 + ,C + 1 = ND44,C1

2. Modeling of Jupiter in Marble in Roman Style

Analysis

Sculpture = ND (CNC)

Italy = 52 [P]

Roman = ,C[P2]

Sky = 28 [P3] to be subdivided as in [P] of B9 Astronomy

Jupiter = 45

Marble = ;3[M]

Modeling = :8 [E]

Synthesis

ND + 52 + ,C + 28 + 45 +;3 + :8 = ND52,C2845;3:8

3. Design of Pallava Bronze Busts

Analysis

Sculpture = ND (CNC)

South India = 441 [P]

Pallava = ,G [P2]

Bust = 18 [P3]

Bronze = ;5 [M]

Design = :4 [E]

Synthesis

ND441 + ,G + 18 + ;5 + ;5 + :4 = ND441, G18;5:4

4. Jain Iconography

Analysis

Sculpture = ND (CNC)

India = 44[P]

Jain = ,[E][P2]

Iconography = 9(Q) [P3]

Synthesis

ND + 44 + ,E + 9 (Q) = ND44,E9(Q)

5. Preservation of human figures in stone

Analysis

Sculpture = ND (CNC)

Human Figure = ,1[P3]

Stone = ;4[M]

Preservation = :98[E]

Synthesis

ND + ,1 + ;4 :98 = ND,1;4:98

10.2.4 NQ Painting

The facet formula for NQ Painting is as follows:

NQ [P],[P2] [P3]; [M]:[E] [2P]

Where foci in [P] = Region To be got by (GD) ⎤ Style

Where foci in [P2] = Epoch to be got by (CD) ⎦

Where foci in [P3] = Figure

Where foci in [M] = Material

Whère foci in [E] = technique

The following are some worked out examples

1. Indian Painting

Analysis

Painting = NQ (CNC)

India = 44 [P] To be got by (CD)

Synthesis

NQ + 44 = NQ44

2. Chalukyan Wood Paintings

Analysis

Painting = NQ (CNC)

Indian = 44[P] to be got by (GD)

Chalukyan = ;D[P2] To be got by (CD)

Wood = ;1[M]

Synthesis

NQ+44+,D+;1 = NQ44,D;1

3. Buddhist fresco colour paintings of animals

Analysis

Painting = NQ (CNC)

India = 44[P] To be got by (GD)

Buddhist = ,C [P2] To be got by (CD)

Animal = 5[P3] As for ND Sculpture

Fresco = ;3 [M]

Colour = :2 [E]

Synthesis

NQ + 44 + ,C + 5 + ;3 + :2 = NQ44,C5;3:2

4. Preservation of Canvas Paintings

Analysis

Painting = NQ (CNC)

Canvas = ;7[M]

Preservation = :98[E]

Synthesis

NQ + ;7 + :98 = NQ;7:98

5. Leonardo Davinci (1502):Mona Lisa

Analysis

Painting = NQ (CNC)

Italy = 52[P] To be got by (GD)

NOTE: As pr rule No9xl (P1.95) the digit x should be amplified by (AD) using the name of the artist. It may be followed by work facet as in O Literature if warranted.

Common Isolate digit = x

Davinci = Davinci

Mona Lisa = 1 (Deemed as first painting work of Davinci)

Synthesis

NQ + 52 + x+ Davinci + 1 = NQ 52x Davinci 1

NOTE: If we apply Classic Device (CLD) the Author Davinci can be represented by (CD) then the class number shall be : NQ52xJo2,1

6. Nandalal Bose (1883): Mahabinishkramana

Analysis

Painting = NQ (CNC)

India = 44[P] To be got by (GD)

Classic Device = x

Nandalal Bose (1883) = M83 [P] To be got by (CD)

Mahebinishkramana = ,1(Deemed as first painting work)

Synthesis

NQ + 44 + x + M83 + ,1 = NQ44xM83,1

10.2.5 NR Music

The facet formula for NR Music is as follows

NR[P], [P2] [P3]; [M] : [E] [2P]

Where foci in [P] = Region To be got by (GD) ⎤ Style

Where foci in [P2] = Epoch To be got by (CD) ⎦

Where foci in [P3] = Music

Where foci in [M] = Instrument

Where foci in [E] [2P] = Technique (To be worked out)

The following are few worked out examples

1. Easy steps in Indian Music

Analysis

Music = NR (CNC)

India = 44 [P] To be got by (GD)

Synthesis

NR + 44 = NR 44

2. Italian Orchestral Music

Analysis

Music	=	NR (CNC)
Italy	=	52 [P] To be got by (GD)
Orchestral Music	=	,92 [P3]

Synthesis

NR + 52 + ,92 = NR52,92

3. Mŕidangaswara bodhini

Analysis

Music	=	NR (CNC)
South	=	441 [P] To be got by (GD)
Swara (Notation)	=	,18[P3]
Mridangam (Percussion Instrument)	=	;4[M]

Synthesis

NR 6+ 441+ ,18 + ;4 = NR 441, 18;4

4. Biography Sri Thyagaraja (1759)

Analysis

Music	=	NR (CNC)
South India	=	441 [P] To be got by (GD)
Vocal Music	=	;91[M]
Biography	=	w (ACI: Applicable only before Space Facet)

Year of Birth of Thyagaraja (1759) = L59[P] To be got by (CD)

Synthesis

NR + 441 +;91 + w + L 59 = NR441;91wL59

5. The unfinished journey, an autobiography of Yehudi Menuhin (1916-1999)

Analysis

Music	=	(CNC)

Britain = 56 [P] To be got by (GD)

Violin = ;32 [M]

Biography = w (ACI: Applicable only Space Facet)

Yehudi Menuhin (1916) = N16 [P] To be got by (CD)

Auto (Biography) = 1, (See facet formula for Autobiography W [P] ,1 at Page 2.5)

Synthesis

NR + 56 +,32+w+N16+,1 = NR56,32wN16,1

Self Check Exercise-1

(a) British Architecture

(b) Architecture of Pallava forts

(c) Elevation of Hellenic theatre pillars

(d) Location of market place in the metropolis

(e) Models of theatres in ancient Roman Cities

(f) Chalukyan style of casting Hindu gods in bronze

(g) The cropus of Anglio-Saxon Stone scriptures

(h) Biography of P.R. Picasso (1881)

(i) Prehistoric Indian rock Painting

(j) Music of Mariam Anderson (1920)

(k) Know your Thyagaraja

(l) The new Oxford Companion to Music, 1983

(m) Nandikeshwara: Abhinaya Darpana

(n) Shadow plays of Indonesia

(o) Marathi Theatre in 1980's

10.3 O LITERATURE

"Writings in prose or verse, esp. writing having excellence of form or expression and expressing ideas of permanent or universal interest." The facet formula for the (MC) O Literature is as follows.

O[P],[P2] [P3], [P4]

Where foci in [P] = Language
Where foci in [P2] = Form
Where foci in [P3] = Author To be got by (CD)
Where foci in [P4] = Work

10.3.1 Rules

Ranganathan has devoted more pages in the theory part of CC (P1-98-1.104) for this (MC) than any other (MC). He has discussed elaborately the four facets that occur in literature i.e. Language [P], Form [P2], Author [P3] and Work [P4]. He has also provided rules and guidelines for classifying documents falling under this (MC). Some of the important rules pertaining to the four facets is presented below:

10.3.1.1 Language Facet

As per rule 1 Language Facet means the language to the literature of which the book belongs or about the literature of which the book treats should be taken as focus in Language Facet.

Eg: 1. Kalidasa's – Sakuntalam – belongs to Sanskrit Literature. Therefore the Language Focus should be Sanskrit eg. 2. Max Miler: Sakuntalam-though it is in English translation, the language focus should be Sanskrit. Because the Original 'Sakuntalam' is in Sanskrit Language. Therefore 'Language of the work' is not equal to 'Language of Book'. CC Provides for 'Local Variation' in the arrangement of books in Literature. As per rule 0164, in the case of Literature in the Favoured Language, the language number should replaced by "———" (Hyphen)

Eg: English poetry 0-,1 instead 0111,1

Shakespeare 0-,2J64 instead 0111,2J64

10.3.1.2 Form Facet

As per rule 02, the Form of Literature which the book contains or about which the book treats should be taken as the focus in the Form Facet

E.g.: English Poetry O111,1

English Drama 0111,2

English Fiction O111,3 and so on

10.3.1.3 Author Facet

As per the rule 031, the author of literary piece or work which the book contains or about which the book treats or the literary author about whom the book treats should be taken as focus in the Author Facet

Eg: 1. Shakespeare: Hamlet. The author is Shakespeare

2. Biography of Shakespeare by Bradley. The author is Shakespeare

3. Criticism of Shakespeare by Bradley. The subject matter of books is Shakespeare and therefore the author is Shakespeare and not Bradley.

As per rule 032, the author (IN) should be constructed by (CD). The (CD) number should be worked out at least to three digits. The year of birth of the author should be used as epoch.

Eg: Rabindranath Tagore (1861) = M61

The arrangement of the authors belonging to particulars Form Isolate may by made either alphabetically or by the name of the author or chronologically. If it is to be on chronological basis there are three main epochs, which can be made the characteristic of Classification.

1. The date of birth of the author
2. The date of which his first Literary work was published
3. The date of death of the author. This is not practicable one, since the date of death of contemporary author is an unknown entity.

10.3.1.4 Work Facet

As per rule 04 the work contained or treated about in the book should be taken as the focus in the Work Facet. Ranganathan has provided the following scheme for the construction of Work Number.

As per rule 041 (1) "If the number of works of the author does not exceed eight the works should by arranged in Chronological sequence or in any arbitrary sequence and the numbers 1,2,3…..8 respectively should be assigned to the works.

As per rule 041 (2) "if the number of works of an author is greater than eight, but does not exceed sixty four, the works should be arranged in chronological sequence or if it is possible in some convenient sequence and they should be divided successively in to groups of eight each, and the numbers 1,2,3….8 respectively should be assigned to the groups of eight each, and the numbers 1,2,3….8 respectively should be put after the Group Number. Thus each work (IN) will consist of two digits, the first digit indicating the group into which the book falls and second indicating the work in the group."

The following table will give us an idea to arrive at work number.

Group No.	No. of works	Sequence of Book No. Written by the Author	Example of Work No.
1.	1-8	4th work	14
2.	9-16	15th work	27
3.	17-24	18th work	32
4.	25-32	27th work	43
5.	33-40	36th work	54
6.	41-48	43rd work	63
7.	49-56	52nd work	74
8.	57-64	62nd work	86

As per rule 041 (3) "if the number works is greater than sixty four but does not exceed 512, the same device may be extended. That is the work (IN) get three digits, the first digit showing the major group by 64 works into which the work falls, the second digit showing the sub-group of the major group in to which the book falls and the third digit indicating the work in the sub0-group''.For example 139 book will get the work No.311 (3 Major Group, 1 Subgroup and 1 the work in the sub group)

It is rather difficult to understand the rationality and usefulness of this method of arriving at work number. The best method is to apply Alphabetical Device by which Individual works of an author can easily be identified and work facet can be represented in the Class Number.

10.3.2 Worked out Examples

The following are some worked out examples

1. An anthology of English Poetry

Analysis

Literature = O (MC)

English = 111[P]

Poetry = ,1[P2]

Anthology = x (ACI – Applicable only before Space Facet)

Synthesis

O + 111 + ,1 + x = O 111, 1x

2. Six famous plays

Analysis

Literature =) (MC)

Plays = ,2[P2]

Collection = x (AC)

Synthesis

O +,2 + x = O,2x

3. Literary Criticism

Analysis

Literature = O (MC)

Criticism = :g (PCI - [E] (CI)

Synthesis

O + g = O:g

4. William Shakespeare (1564): Hamlet

Analysis

Literature = O (MC)

English = 111[P]

Drama = ,2[P2]

Shakespeare (1564) = J64 [P3] To be got by (CD)

Hamlet = ,1 [P4] Treated as his first work

Synthesis

O + 111 +,2 +J64 + ,1 = O111, 2J64,1

5. Rabindranath Tagore (1861): Gitanjali

Literature = O(MC)

Bengali = 157[P]

Poetry = ,1 [P2]

Tagore (1861) = M61 [P3] To be got by (CD)

Gitanjali = ,1 P[P4] Treated as his first work

Synthesis

O157 + ,1 + M61 + ,1 = O157, 1M61,1

6. Borris Pasternak (1890):Dr. Zhivago

Analysis

Literature = O (MC)

Russian = 142 [P]

Fiction = ,3 [P2]

Pasternak (1890) = M90 [P3] To be got by (CD)

Dr. Zhivago = , 1[P4] Treat as his first work

Synthesis

O + 142 + ,3 M90 + ,1 = O142, 3M90,1

7. Gurazada Appa Rao (1861): Kanyasulkam

Analysis

Literature = O (MC)

Telugu = 35[P]

Drama = ,2[P2]

Appa Rao (1861) = M61[P3] To be got by (CD)

Kanyasulkam = ,1[P4] Treat as his first work

Synthesis

O +\ 35 + ,2 M61 + ,1 =)35,2M61,1

8. Kalidas (40 AD): Sakuntalam

Analysis

Literature	= O(MC)
Sanskrit	= 15 [P]
Drama	= ,2 [P2]
Kalidas (40 AD)	= D 40 [P3] To be got by (CD)
Sakuntalam	= ,1[P4] Treated as his first work

Synthesis

O + 15 + ,2 D40 + ,1 = O15, 2D40,1

9. Criticism of Sumitranandan Pant's (1900) Poetry

Analysis

Literature	= O (MC)
Hindi	= 152 [P]
Poetry	= ,1[P2]
Pant (1900)	= N00[P3] To be got by (CD)
Criticism	= :g (PCI-[E](CI)

Synthesis

O + 152 + ,1 + N00 + :g = O152,1N00:g

10. Biography of Mark Twain (1835)

Analysis

Literature	= O(MC)
English	= 111 [P]

NOTE: Mark Twain is an American Novelist. But the language spoken in USA is English or American English. In CC there is no distinction between British English, American English or Indian English. Therefore we have to use 111 to represent English Language in [P]

Fiction	= ,3[P2]
Mark Twain (1835)	= M35 [P3] To be got by (CD)
Biography	= w (ACI-Applicable before Space Facet)

Synthesis

O + 111 +,3 M35 + w = O111,3M35w

Self Check Exercise-2

(a) Poetry of Mathew Arnold (1822)
(b) J.B.P. Moilere (1622): Misanthrope; a comedy 13th Work)
(c) Omar Khayam (1025): Rubayats (4th Work)
(d) Herman Heses (1877): The Prodigy (15th Work)
(e) Saratchandra Chattopadhyaya (1876): Devadas (18th work)
(f) Viswanadha Satya Narayana (1895): Veipadagalu (12th Work)
(g) V.K. Gokak (1923) Kashmira, a collection of Poetry
(h) The Concise Oxford Dictionary of Literary terms, 1990
(i) Comparative Literature and literary history
(j) Journal of Semitic studies, 1985
(k) A short history of modern Arabic Literature
(l) Girish Karnad (1938) Naga Mandala: Play with a Cobra (First work)

10.4 P LINGUISTICS

"The study of human speech including the units, nature, structure and modification of Language." The facet formula for P Linguistics is as follows:

P[P],[P][P3] :[E][2P]

Where foci in [P] = Language
Where foci in [P2] = Variant, Stage
Where foci in [P3] = Element
Where foci in [E] [2P] = Problem

10.4.1 Rules

Before we proceed to some of the important rules provided for Linguistics in theory of Part of C (Pl.105-1.107) let us understand the meaning some important words, which we come across in Linguistics.

Slang = The Jargon of any class, profession

or sect, Colloquial Language.

Dialect = Variety or form of a language peculiar to a district or class.

Jargon = The technical terminology or Characteristic idiom of a special activity or group.

Variant = Different from the same thing

As per rule P290 if a book treats variant of a language such as dialects or a slang or jargon, the language number should be divided by the addition of appropriate number taken from the list of Variants given in chapter P of the schedules (P2.95)

Eg: 1. English Slang P111, 9B

2. French Dialect P122, 9D

As per rule P2901 "Comma should separate the variant facet and [P3]"

3. Words in English Slang P111, 9B,3

As per rule 929D, "if the book treats a specific dialect peculiar to a definite geographic division, the dialect number may be further divided by the addition of the Geographical Number appropriate to the area in which it is current".

4. Yorkshire Dialect P111, 9D 56175 (Yorkshire taken from Space Isolate)

5. Ardhamagadhi dialect in Hindi P152, 9D 4473 (Bihar Taken from Space Isolate)

As per rule P29J, "after the Jargon number, the Geographical Number and Century Number corresponding to the place and period of Origin of the Jorgon may be put if necessary. A comma should separate the (GN) and Century Number"

6. Anglo-Indian jargon P111,,9J44 → Century Number

↓

Geographic Number

As per rule P29Z, "if both Stage Number and Variant Number are warranted the Variant Number should follow the Stage Number'; and a Comma should separate them".

7. Modern Yorkshire dialect P111,J,9D 56175

↓ ↓

Stage Variant

As per rule P2A0A "in the case of books dealing with the grammar of single Veda, the stage digit 'A' should be preceded by a number, the first digit representing the Veda and the latter digits, the recession concerned''

8. Vedic Kanva Sanskrit P15, 28A (28 Kanva, taken from [P] of Q Religion)

As per rule P2AoA "if a book deals with more than one recession of Veda, the second digit or the Recession digit as it may be called should be zero. The Veda digit and the recession digit should be taken from Chapter Q of the Schedules''

9. Language of Samaveda P15,30A (13 Samaveda. Taken from [P] of Q Religion)

As per rule P44, "if the Problem Number is '4' or '5' or subdivision of '5' and if the elements is '3' the Element Number may be omitted''.

10. English Language Dictionary P111,3:4k. But according to the above rule the Class Number should be P111:4k

As per rule P48 "a dictionary of Special Terms used in a particular subject should be placed in the subject concerned and its number should be got by (SD). That is, a Colon should be put after the number representing the particular science or subject and thereafter P followed by the number of the language concerned should be added within circular brackets''.

11. Library Science glossary in Telugu 2: (P35)

12. Physics terms in urdu C:(P168)

As per rule P9k "in case of ordinary dictionaries giving the meaning of words, phrases, idioms and proverbs, the language part of the Book Number should represent the language in which the meaning is given in two or more languages.

13. English-French Dictionary (1960) P111:4k ←Class Number

122KO ← Book Number

14. Hindi-Telugu Dictionary (1966) P152:4k ← Class Number
35K6 ← Book Number

As per rule P9(G) "if the main purpose of a book that of giving not a descriptive but a comparative account, its class number should be worked out to the fullest extent and ''(G)'' should be added thereafter''

15. Comparative study of African Language P6(G)
16. Comparative study of grammar of African Languages P6:2(G)

10.4.2 Worked out Examples

The following are few more worked out examples, with analysis and synthesis of Class Numbers

1. Modern Yorkshire Dialect

Analysis

Linguistics = P(MC)
English = 111[P]
Modern = ,J Variant [P2]
Dialect = 9D Stage
Yorkshire = 56163 Taken from [S]

Synthesis

P + 111 + ,J + 9D + 56163 = P111,J9D56163

2. Dictionary of Anglo Indian Jargon

Analysis

Linguistics = P(MC)
English = 111[P]
Jargon = ,9J[P2]
India = 44 Taken from [S]
Period (18th Century) = ,L (See rule P29J)
Meaning (for a given element) = :4 [E] [2P]
Dictionary = k (ACI-Applicable before Space Facet)

Synthesis

P + 111 + ,9J + 44 + ,L + :4 + k = P111,9J44, L: 4k

3. Telugu-Hindi Dictionary

Analysis

Linguistics = P(MC)

Telugu = 35 [P]

Meaning = :4 [E] [2P]

Dictionary = k (ACI)

Synthesis

P + 35 + :4 + k = P35:4k

NOTE: In case of bilingual dictionaries the second language in which the meaning is given is to be shown in Book Number. See rule P9k (P1.106)

4. Madras Hindi Reader standard 4.1960

Analysis

Linguistics = P (MC)

Hindi = 152 [P]

Reader = ,9[P3]

Standard 4 = (4)

Synthesis

P + 152 + ,9 + (4) + N60 = P152,9(4)N60

5. Comparative study of pronouns in Indo European languages

Analysis

Linguistics = P (MC)

Indo-European = 1[P]

Pronouns = ,34 [P3]

Comparative study = (G) see rule P9(G)

Synthesis

P + 1 + , 34 (G) = P1,34 (G)

6. Introduction to Classical Sanskrit Grammar

Analysis

Linguistics = P(MC)

Sanskrit = 15 [P]

Classical (Stage) = ,C [P2]

Grammar = :2 [E] [2P]

Synthesis

P + 15 + ,C + :2 = p 15,C:2

7. Stevensons Book of Quotations

Analysis

Linguistics = P(MC)

English = 111[P]

Quotation = ,6[P3]

Dictionary = k(ACI)

Synthesis

P + 111 + ,6 + k = P111,6k

8. Telugu Typewriting Practice book, grade 4, 1966.

Typewriting = P(6) Special

Telugu = 35 [P]

Materials for practice = ,9

Grade 4 = (4)

1966 = N66

Synthesis

P (6) + 35 + ,9 (4) + N66 = P35,9 (4) N66

9. Pitaman's Shorthand book, grade 2,1960

Analysis

Shorthand = P(3) Special

English = 111[P]

Materials for practice = ,9 [P3]

Grade 2 = (2)

1960 = N60

Synthesis

P (3) + 111 +,9 + (2) + N60 = P (3) 111,9 (2) N60

10. International Encyclopedia of linguistics, 1992

Analysis

Linguistics = P(MC)

Encyclopedia = k (ACI)

International (world) = 1 [P]

1992 = ,N92 [P2]

Synthesis

P + k + 1 + , N92 = Pk1, N92

Self Check Exercise-3

(a) Pronunciation in Modern Lancashire dialect

(b) Structure of Verbs in Classical Sanskrit

(c) Treatment of genders in Old Kanarese

(d) Semaisiology of dialects in Coastal Andhra

(e) Telugu Story reader standard 6.1992

(f) History of modern American slang

(g) Synthesis of sentences in modern French

(h) Hindi Typewriting Practice Book grade (4) 1992

(i) A practical introduction to phonetics

(j) The Oxford Dictionary of Modern Slang, 1992

(k) A Sanskrit Grammar for students

(l) Comparative Dictionary of Indo-Aryan Languages 1966.

10.5 Q RELIGION

"A personal set or institutionalized system of religious attitudes, beliefs and practices''. The facet formula for Q Religion is as follows.

Q [P]:[E] [2P]

Where foci in [P] = Religion To be got by enumeration and also by (GD) and (CD)

`Where foci in [E] [2P] = Problem

The following are few worked out examples.

1. Sacred books in Vaisanavism

Analysis

Religion = Q (MC)

Vaisnavism = 22[P]
Sacred books = :2 [E] [2P]
Synthesis
Q + 22 + :2 = Q22:2

2. Christian Mythology
Religion = Q (MC)
Christianity = 6 [P]
Mythology = :1 [E] [2P]
Synthesis
Q + 6 + :1 = Q6:1

3. Sayings of Islam
Analysis
Religion = Q (MC)
Islam = 7 [P]
Sayings = :25 [E] [2P]
Synthesis
Q + 7 + : 25 = Q7:25

4. Rigveda Samhita
Analysis
Religion = Q (MC)
Rigveda = 11 [P]
Samhita = :21[E][2P]
Synthesis
Q + 11 + :21 = Q11 :21

5. Rebirth according to Hinayana Buddhism
Analysis
Religion = Q (MC)
Hinayana = 41[P]
Rebirth = :366 [E] [2P]
Synthesis
Q + 41 + :366 = Q41:366

6. Preachings in Judaism

   Analysis

   Religion = Q (MC)

   Judaism = 5 [P]

   Preachings = :51[E] [2P]

   Synthesis

   Q + 5 + :51 = Q5:51

7. Biography of Raja Ram Mohan Roy (1774-1883)

   Analysis

   Religion = Q (MC)

   Bramosamaj = 29M2 [P]

   Biography = w

   Raja Rama Mohan Roy (1774) = L74 [P] by (CD)

   Synthesis

   Q + 29M2 + w + L74 = Q29M2 wL74

8. An Introduction to Philosophy of Religion

   Analysis

   Religion = Q (MC)

   Philosophy = : (R) (MC) To be got by (SD)

   Synthesis

   Q + : (R) = Q : (R)

Self Check Exercise-4

(a) A short history of Christian thought

(b) Religion and Science

(c) Biblical faith and national Theology

(d) Images of Buddha in Thailand

(e) Organising Jainism in India and England

(f) Siva in Dance, Myth and Iconography

(g) Journal of Islamic studies, Lord on 1990

(h) Jewish social ethics

(i) Korea: A Religious History

(j) A History of Reform movement in Judaism

10.6 R PHILOSOPHY

"A search for truth through logical reasoning rather than factual observation''. It is further divided on Canonical lines. The following are Canonical divisions of Philosophy.

R1	Logic
R2	Epistemology
R3	Metaphysics
R4	Ethics
R5	Aesthetics
R6	Indian Philosophy (Favoured System 1)
R7	Favoured System (2)
R8	Other Systems by (GD)

For some of the Canonical divisions we find facet formula.

10.6.1 R3 Metaphysics

The facet formula for R3 Metaphysics is as follows:

R3[P],[P2]

Where foci in[P] = View

Where foci in [P2] = Subject, To be got by (SD)

The following are few worked out examples.

1. Rationalism

Analysis

Metaphysics = R3 (CNC)

Rationalism = 4 [P]

Synthesis

R3 + 4 = R34

2. Radical humanism

Analysis

Metaphysics = R3 (CNC)

Humanism = 9 (Y) [P]

Synthesis

R 3 + 9 (Y) = R39 (Y)

3. Biography of MN Roy (1890)

   Analysis

   Metaphysics = R3 (CNC)

   Humanism = 9(Y) [P]

   Biography = w (ACI)

   MN Roy = M90 [P] To be got by (CD)

   Synthesis

   R3 +9(Y) + w + M90 = R39 (Y) w M90

4. Judaistic Philosophy

   Analysis

   Metaphysics = R3 (CNC)

   Judaism = ,(Q5) [P2] To be got by (SD)

   Synthesis

   R3 + ,(Q5) + R3, (Q5)

5. Metaphysical theory of gold

   Analysis

   Metaphysics = R3 (CNC)

   Gold = ,(E118) [P2] To be got by (SD)

   Synthesis

   R3 + ,(E118) = R3, (E118)

10.6.2 R4 Ethics

The facet formula for R4 Ethics is as follows:

R4[P],[P2]

Where foci in [P] = Topic

Where foci in [P2] = Controlling Principle. Other division to be got by (SD)

The following are worked out examples

1. Social Ethics

Analysis

Ethics = R4 (CNC)

Social = 3[P]

Synthesis

R4 + 3 = R43

2. Marriage ethics of Hindus

Analysis

Ethics = R4 (CNC)

Marriage = 217 [P]

Hinduism = ,(Q2) [P2] To be got by (SD)

Synthesis

R4 + 217 + ,(Q2) = R4 217, (Q2)

3. Medical Ethics

Analysis

Ethics = R4 (CNC)

Professional Ethics = 4[P]

Medicine = ,(L) [P2] To be got by (SD)

Synthesis

R4 + 4 + ,(L) = R44, (L)

4. Ethics of Chess

Analysis

Ethics = R4 (CNC)

Ethics of lensure = 6[P] To be divided as MY

Chess = 322

Synthesis

R4 + 6 + 322 = R4 6322

5. Conduct towards animals according to Buddhists

Analysis

Ethics = R4 (CNC)

Conduct towards animals = 6 [P]

Buddhism = ,(Q4) [P2]

Synthesis

R4 + 6 + ,(Q4) = R46, (Q4)

10.6.2.1 R6 Indian Philosophy

The facet formula for R6 Indian Philosophy is as follows:

R6[P], [P2] [P3], [P4]

Where foci in [P] = System

Where foci in[P2] = Basic text

Where foci in [P3] = Author by Classic Device (CLD)

Where foci in [P4] = Work

The following are worked out examples:

1. Hindu Philosophy

Analysis

Indian Philosophy = R6 (CNC)

Hindu = 1[P]

Synthesis

R6 + 1 = R61

2. Yoga Philosophy

Analysis

Indian Philosophy = R6 (CNC)

Yoga = 35 [P]

Synthesis

R6 + 35 = R635

3. Upanishads

Analysis

Indian Philosophy = R6

Vedanta = 5[P]

Upanishad = ,0[P2]

Synthesis

R6 + 5 + ,0 = R65,0

4. Bhaskarabhatta (1995): Bhatta Chandrika

Analysis

Indian Philosophy = R6 (CNC)

Bhattamimasa = 41 [P]

Classic Device = x (ACI)

Bhaskarabhatta (1695)= K95 [P3] (To be got by (CD))

Bhattachandrika = ,1[P4] Treated as first work

Synthesis

R6 + 41 + x + k95 + ,1 = R641 xK95,1

5. Ramadasa (1608): Dasa bodha

Analysis

Indian Philosophy = R6 (CNC)

Vedanta = 5 [P]

Classic Device = x (ACI)

Ramadasa (1608) = K08 [P3] To be got by (CD)

Dasa bodha = ,1 [P4] Treated as first work

Synthesis

R6 + 5 + ,x + K08 + ,1 = R65xK08,1

10.6.3 R8 Other Systems of Philosophy

The followings are worked out examples of other systems of Philosophy

1. British Philosophy

Analysis

Other Systems = R8

British = 56 (GD)

Synthesis

R8 + 56 = R856

2. German Philosophy

Analysis

Other Systems = R8

German = 55 (GD)

Synthesis

R8 + 55 = R855

3. Bertrand Russell (1872): Collected Works

   Analysis

   British Philosophy = R856
   Collected works = x (ACI)
   Russell (1872) = M72 To be got by (CD)

   Synthesis

   R856 +x+M72 = R856xM72

4. Henry James (1811): Relation to life

   Analysis

   American Philosophy = R 873
   Classic Device = x (ACI)
   Henry James (1811) = M11 [P3] To be got by (CD)
   Relation to life = ,1[P4] Treated as first work

   Synthesis

   R873+x+M11+,1 = R873xM11,1

5. Plato (42.7MC): The Republic

   Analysis

   Greek Philosophy = R 851
   Classic Device = x (ACI)
   Plato (427BC) = C572[P3] To be got by (CD)
   Republic = ,1[P4] Treated as first work

   Synthesis

   R851+x+C572+,1 = R851x572,1

Self Check Exercise-5

(a) Theory of Knowledge
(b) Ethics of democracy'
(c) Mahayana Philosophy
(d) Bhagavadgita
(e) Sankara: Brahmasutra Bhasya
(f) Kant (1724): Critique of pure reason

(g) George Santayana (1863): Platonism and spiritual life

(h) The British journal of Aesthetics 1960

(i) Principles of Biomedical Ethics

(j) The meaning of life

(k) The development of logic

(l) J.J. Rousseau (1712-1778): The Social Contract

10.7 SUMMARY

In the preceeding sections we have introduced you to the art and technique of classifying titles under Humanities. The (MCs) filling under this partial comprehension are: N Fine Arts, O Literature, R Philosophy P Linguistics, Q Religion and R Philosophy. The facet formula provided for each of the (MCs) including those of canonical divisions are explained and well supported by worked out examples. The relevant rules form part I of CC have been cited to articulate the intricacies in the construction of Class Number or Number building. The occurrence of each facet in a given title has been analysed citing the relevant focal numbers from the schedules and synthesized to arrive at Coextensive Class Number. Through Self-Check Exercises provided for under each (MC) you will have ample opportunity for classifying documents with CC. This practice would keep you in good stead to apply various rules and techniques of classification presented in Part I of CC.

10.8 ANSWERS TO SELF-CHECK EXERCISE

Exercise-1

(a) NA56

(b) NA441,G37

(c) NA51,c8(NT),45:4

(d) NB,7,5:1

(e) NB52,D5,691:8

(f) ND44,D8(Q2:31);5:5

(g) ND561,D;4

(h) NQ541urM81

(i) NQ44,B;4

(j) NR73;91xN20

(k) NR441;91xL59:g

(l) NRk56,N83

(m) NS44x1,1

(n) NV436

(o) NT4435'N8

Exercise-2

(a) O111,M22

(b) O122,2K22,25

(c) O164,1E25,14

(d) O113,3M77,27

(e) O157,3M76,32

(f) O35,3M95,24

(g) O33,1N23x

(h) O(P111)k56,N90

(i) O(G)OaOs

(j) O2m56,N85

(k) O28s,

(l) O33,2N38,1

Exercise-3

(a) P111,J,9D 56163,1:1

(b) P15,C35:2

(c) P33,E:22

(d) P35,9D4418:4

(e) P35,9(6)w3N92

(f) P111,J,9Bv

(g) P122,H6:291

(h) P (6)152,9(4) N92

(i) P:1

(j) P111,J,9Bk56,N92

(k) P15:2ObT

(l) P1:(G)k56,N66

Exercise-4

(a) R6v

(b) QOaA

(c) Q6:3

(d) Q4:415,433

(e) Q3.44Oj561

(f) Q23:1

(g) Q7m56,N90

(h) Q5(R43)

(i) Qv495

(j) Q5v

Exercise-5

(a) R2

(b) R43w6

(c) R6945

(d) R65,6

(e) R66,5x1,1

(f) R855xL24,1

(g) R873xM63,1

(h) R5m56,N60

(i) R4:(G:(L))

(j) R3

(k) R1v

(l) R853xL12,1

10.8 ASSIGNMENT

Assign Class Numbers to the following titles:

1. Sanskrit drama in its origin and development

2. Early Buddhism and Christianity, a Comparative study'
3. A concordance to the principal Upanishads and Bhagavad-Gita
4. The Dictionary of Hindustani Classical Music
5. The poems of Suradasa
6. Comparative study of the Indo-Aryan Languages
7. An outline history of Saiva Philosophy
8. A Grammar of Prakrit Language
9. Vedic Mathematics for Schools
10. Arts and Crafts of North India
11. The Buddhist Arts of Gandhara
12. Dances of India: A General survey and dancers guide
13. Encyclopedia of Religion and Ethics
14. Dictionary of Telugu-English
15. A Dictionary of Philosophy

UNIT 11
Main Classes Under Social Sciences

11.0 OBJECTIVES

In unit 10, we have introduced you to the art of Classification of titles under Humanities. In this Unit, we will introduce you to the classification of titles under Social Sciences. After going through this unit you should be able to:

- Understand the rules of classification pertaining to (MCs) under Social Sciences
- Know the facet formula of each of the (MC) and its implications, and
- Assign Class Number to titles falling under the (MCs) S Psychology, T Education, U Geography, V History, W Political Science, X Economics, Y Sociology and Z Law.

11.1 INTRODUCTION

In unit 10 we have introduced you to classify documents under Humanities. In this unit we will introduce you to classify documents under Social Sciences. The Main Classes (MCs) which broadly come under Social Sciences are: S Psychology, T Education, U Geography, V History, W Political Science, X Economics, Y Sociology and Z Law. Each (MC) will be introduced to you citing its facet formula, explaining the implications of each facet, and relevant and important rules stated in Part I of CC, and well demonstrated by worked out examples. Let us take up each one of the (MCs) under Social Sciences.

11.2 S PSYCHOLOGY

"The Science of mind or mental phenomena; systematic knowledge about mental process''. The facet formula for S Psychology is as follows:

S[P]: [E][2P]

Where foci in [P] = Entity

Where foci in [E][2P] = Problem

The following are worked out examples

1. Child Psychology

Analysis

Psychology = S (MC)

Child = 1[P]

Synthesis

S + 1= S1

As per rule S14, Page 1.112 "the division '4 vocational' should include classes of persons belonging to different vocations and thus may be subdivided by (SD)''

2. Psychology of Engineers

Analysis

Psychology = S (MC)

Vocational = 4 [P]

Engineers = (D) To be got by (SD)

Synthesis

S + 4 + (D) = S4 (D)

3. Psychology of Genius

Analysis

Psychology = S (MC)

Genius = 61 [P]

Synthesis

S + 61 = S61

As per rule S17, Page 1.112 "the division '7 Race' may, whenever necessary be subdivided as Y7 Sociology"

4. Psychology of Hindus

Analysis

Psychology = S (MC)

Hindu = 73 (Q2) [P] Taken from [P] of Y Sociology

Synthesis

S + 73 (Q2) = S73 (Q2)

5. Psychological reactions of human Brain

Analysis

Psychology = S (MC)

Nervous System = :1 [E] [2P] To be divided as [P] 7 of L Medicine

Brain = 72 from [P] of L Medicine

Synthesis

S + 1:1 + 2 = S:12

6. Interpretation of dreams among children

Analysis

Psychology = S (MC)

Child = 1 [P]

Dream = :811 [E] [2P]

Synthesis

S + 1 + :811 = S1 : 811

7. A Guide to happiness

Analysis

Psychology = S (MC)

Happiness = :51

Synthesis

S + 51 = S : 51

8. Psychology of habits among Old Persons

Analysis

Psychology = S(MC)

Old Person = 38 [P]

Habit = :35 [E] [2P]

Psychometry = :6[2E][3Psychology] for 2 and 3 of [E]

Synthesis

S + 38 + :35 +:6 = S38:35:6

9. Psychoanalysis of Personality

Analysis

Psycho-analysis = SM9 (System)

Personality = :7 [E] [2P]

Synthesis

SM9+:7 = SM9:7

10. Behaviouristic Psychology of Joy of adolescents

Analysis

Behaviouristic Psychology = SN1 (System)

Adolescent = ,2[P] To be added with coma (See rule SA, P1.112)

Joy = :523[E][2P]

Synthesis

SN1+,2+:523 = SN1,2:523

Self Check Exercise-1

(a) Psychology of Librarians

(b) Psychology o Russians

(c) Anger of Women

(d) Dale Carnegie: How to win friends and influence people

(e) Anatomy of smell among girls

(f) Psychoanalysis of emotions among males

(g) The Psychology of meditation

(h) A Practical guide to behaviour research

(i) Research in Experimental Psychology

(j) Research methods in Educational Psychology

11.3 T EDUCATION

"The act or process of providing with knowledge, skill, competence or usually desirable qualities of behaviour or character or of being so provided especially by a formal course of study, institution training etc." The facet formula for T Education is as follows:

T [P]:[E][2P],[2P2]

Where foci in [P] = Education

Where foci in [E] = Problem

Where foci in [2P] = Subject for 3 teaching techniques, 4 curriculum and 5 educational measurement in [E]

Where foci in [2P2] = Method

The following are worked out examples:

1. Secondary Education in India

Analysis

Education = T (MC)

Secondary = 2[P]

India = .44[S]

Synthesis

T + 2 + 44 = T2.44

2. Rural education in Andhra Pradesh

Analysis

Education = T (MC)

Rural = 9 (Y310)[P]

Andhra Pradesh = .4416 [S]

Synthesis

T+9(Y31)+.4416 = T9(Y31).4416

3. Place of Curriculum in Elementary education

Analysis

Education = T (MC)

Elementary = 15[P]

Curriculum = :2[E]

Synthesis

T + 15 + :2 = T15:2.

4. Algebra Curriculum in Secondary Schools

Analysis

Education = T (MC)

Secondary = 2[P]

Curriculum = :2[E]

Algebra = (B2) [2P] By (SD)

Synthesis

T + 2 + :2+(B2) = T2:2 (BC)

5. Visual method of teaching

Analysis

Education = T (MC)

Teaching = :3[E]

Visual Method = ,15 [2P2] for 3 of [E]

Synthesis

T + :3 + ,15 = T:3,15

6. Audio-Visual method of teaching Physics in Secondary Schools

Analysis

Education = T (MC)

Secondary School = 2[P]

Teaching technique = :3[E]

Physics = (C) [2P] By (SD)

Audio-Visual method = ,1[2P2] for 3 of [E]

Synthesis

T +2+ :3 + (C) +,1 = T2:3(C),1

7. Mathematics competition among PG students

Analysis

Education = T (MC)

PG Students = 45 [P]

Student work = :4[E]

Mathematics = (B) [2P] By (SD)

Competition = ,6 [2P2] for 4 of [E]

Synthesis

T + 45 + :4 + (B) + ,6 = T45:4 (B),6

8. **Teaching of mother tongue in Secondary Schools in Karnataka**

Analysis

Education = T(MC)

Secondary School = 2[P]

Teaching Technique = :3[E]

Mother Tongue = (P1)[2P] By (SD) see rule T3 (P1.113)

Karnataka = .4413

Synthesis

T + 2 + :3 (P1)+.4413 = T2:3(P1).4413

9. **Methods of teaching Indian History in Basic Secondary schools in India**

Analysis

Basic (Education) = TN3 (System)

Secondary School = 2[P]

Teaching Technique = :3[E]

Indian History = (V44) [2P] By (SD)

India = .44[S]

Synthesis

TN3+,2+:3+(V44)+.44 = TN3,2:3 (V44).44

10. Inspection of elementary schools in Tamilnadu

Analysis

Education = T (MC)

Elementary School = 15 [P]

Management = :8 [E] To be divided further as in [E] of X Economics

Inspection = 9S

Tamilnadu = .4411

Synthesis

T+15+:8+9S+.4411 = T15:89S.4411

Self Check Exercise-2

(a) Education of refugees in India
(b) Place of Algebra in the curriculum
(c) Audio-Visual method of teaching in elementary schools
(d) Teaching Library & Information Science in the Universities by lecture method
(e) Teaching foreign language in colleges
(f) Library work for university students
(g) Teaching techniques in Montessori Schools
(h) Audio-Visual method of teaching Algebra in Basic Secondary schools in India in 1960's
(i) Management of Vocational Education in India
(j) History of Osmania University (1918) Hyderabad
(k) Kothari commission Report, 1966
(l) Directory of Scientific and Research Institution in India, New Delhi, INSDOC, 1969.

11.4 U GEOGRAPHY

"A science that deals with the earth and its life especially the description of land, sea and the distribution of plant and animal life including man and his industries''

The facet formula for U Geography is as follows:

U[P].[S][T]

Where foci in [P] = Type of Geography
Where foci in [S] = Space
Where foci in [T] = Time

The following are worked out examples

1. Research in Meteorology

Analysis

Geography = U (MC)

Meteorology = 28 [P]

Research = :f(PCI-[E])

Synthesis

U + 28 + :f = U28:f

2. Rainfall atlas of Assam

Analysis

Geography = U(MC)

Rainfall = 2885[P]

Atlas = f (ACI-Applicable before space facet)

Assam = 4477 [S]

Synthesis

U + 2885 + f + 4477 = U2885 f 4477

3. Travels in India during 1980's

Analysis

Geography = U(MC)

Travel = 8[P]

India = .44[S]

1980's = 'N8[P]

Synthesis

U + 8 + 44 + 'N8 = U8.44'N8

4. Adventures of Antarctic expeditions in 1930's

Analysis

Geography = U (MC)

Expedition = 8[P]

Antarctic = .983[S]

1930's = 'N3[T]

Synthesis

U + 8 + .983 + 'N3 = U8.983'N3

5. The Oxford Economic Altas of the world

Geography = U (MC)

Economic = 6[P]

Atlas = f (ACI-Applicable before Space Facet)

World = 1[S]

Synthesis

U+66+f+1 = U6f1

6. Frontier on the Riogrande, a Political Geography

Analysis

Geography = U (MC)

Political = 5[P]

USA = .73 [S]

Synthesis

U+5+.7= U5.73

Self Check Exercise-3

(a) Soils and Geomorphology

(b) The Geography of British Heavy Industry since 1800

(c) The story of a Journey in the inner Himalayas

(d) Early maps of South-East Asia

(e) A Geography of Pakistan

(f) Biography of Ronald Amundsen (1872-1928)

11.5 V HISTORY

"A systematic account of the origin and progress of the world, nation and an institution, a chronological record of significant events effecting a nation, institution,''. The facet formula for V History is as follows:

V[P],[P2]:[E] [2P] '[T]

Where foci in [P] = Community. To be got by (GD)

Where foci in [P2] = Part

Where foci in [E][2P] = Problem

Where foci in [T] = Time

1. History of India

Analysis

History = V (MC)

India = 44[P] To be got by (GD)

Synthesis

V + 44 = V44

2. British Empire

History = V (MC)

World = 1

Britain = -56[P] To be got by (GD) and (SID)

Synthesis

V + 1 + -56 = V1-56

3. History of British India

Analysis

History = V (MC)

India = 44

Britain = -56[P] To be got by (GD) and (SID)

Synthesis

V + 44+-56 = V44-56

4. Indian Parliament

Analysis

History = V(MC)

India = 44[P] To be got by (GD)

Parliament = ,3[P2]

Synthesis

V + 44 + ,3 = V44,3

5. Local bodies in Andhra Pradesh

Analysis

History = V (MC)

Andhra Pradesh = 4416 [P] To be got by (GD)

Local body = ,6[P2]

Synthesis

V + 4416 + ,6 = V4416,6

6. Adhoc body for Public Health of local bodies in India

Analysis

History = V(MC)

India = 44[P] To be got by (GD)

Adhoc Local body = ,68[P2]

Public Health = (L:5) To be got by (SD)

Synthesis

V + 44 + ,68 + (L:5) = V44,68 (L:5)

Foreign Policy

In the annexure to CC we find special facet formula and revised schedule for Foreign Policy (P25 and 28). We have to use this revised schedule for classifying documents dealing with foreign policy.

7. India's Foreign Policy

Analysis

History = V(MC)

India = 44[P] To be got by (GD)

Foreign Policy = 19[E][2P]

Synthesis

V + 44 + :19 = V44:19

8. India's Non-Aligned Policy

Analysis

History = V (MC)

India = 44[P] To be got by (GD)

Non-Aligned Policy = :19 (zk) [E][2P]

Synthesis

V + 44 + :19(zk) = V44:19(zk)

9. China's Foreign Policy towards USA brought up to 1990's

Analysis

History = V (MC)

China = 41[P] To be got by (GD)

Foreign Policy = :19[E]

USA = 73 [P] (Community) See rule V319.1 at P.25 of the Annexure

1990's = 'N9[T]

Synthesis

V + 41 + :19 + 73 + 'N9 = V44:1973 'N9

10. India's trade policy towards Russia brought up to 1990's

Analysis

History = V(MC)

India = 44[P] To be got by (GD)

Foreign Policy = 19[E]

Russia = 47[P]

Trade = ,(X:5) [P2] See rules V3191 and V3192 at page 25 of the Annexure

1990's = 'N9[T]

Synthesis

V + 44 + :19 + 47 + , (X:5) + 'N9 + V44:1947, (X:5)'N9

As per rule V9y7 (Annexure Page 25) "the (CN) for the biography of a person whose importance due to the part played by him in the development of history of a geographical area should be got by adding the (ACIN) "y7" after the Community (IN) and by Sharpening it by (CD), the epoch used being his year of birth".

11. Autobiography of Jawaharlal Nehru (1889)

Analysis

History = V (MC)

India = 44 [P] To be got by (GD)

Case study = y7 (ACI)

Nehru (1889) = M89 [P] To be got by (CD)

Autobiography = ,1

Synthesis

V + 44 + y7 + M89 + ,1 = V44y7M89,1

12. Biography of Mahatma Gandhi (1869)

Analysis

History = V (MC)

India = 44 [P] To be got by (GD)

Case study = y7 (ACI)

Gandhi (1869) = M69 [P] To be got by (CD)

Synthesis

V ++ 44 + y7 M69 = V44y7M69

13. Indian Epigraphy

Analysis

History = V(MC)

India = 44[P] To be got by (GD)

Epigraphy = :72[E][2P]

Synthesis

V + 44 + :72 = V44:72

14. Freedom movement in Angola

Analysis

History = V (MC)

Angola = 643 [P] To be got by (GD)

Freedom Movement = :51 [E][2P]

Synthesis

V + 643 + :51 = V643:51

Self Check Exercise-4

(a) Lok Sabha

(b) Functions of Prime Minister of India

(c) Foreign Policy between Russia and UK

(d) Life of Dr. Rajendra Prasad (1886)

(e) The Philosophy of History

(f) International yearbook of Oral History 1992

(g) Nehru: Glimpses of World History

(h) India-China cultural relations

(i) Chronology of important events: India, 1947-1997

(j) Epigraphical study of Rajasthan inscriptions

11.6 W POLITICAL SCIENCE

"A Social Science concerned chiefly with the description and analysis of political especially governmental institutions and processes and making use of factual material and methods selected from Social Sciences''. The facet formula for W Political Science is as follows:

W[P],[P2]:[E][2P]

Where foci in [P] = Type of state

Where foci in [P2] = Part

Where foci in[E][2P] = Problem

(Same as for V History)

The following are few worked out examples:

1. Introduction to Democracy

Analysis

Political Science = W (MC)

Democracy = 6[P]

Synthesis

W + 6 = W6

2. Functions of a President in democratic state

Analysis

Political Science = W (MC)

Democracy = 6[P]

President = ,1[P2]

Functions = :3 [E] [2P]

Synthesis

W + 6 + ,1 + :3 = W6,1:3

3. Civil rights and duties in a Communist state

Analysis

Political Science = W (MC)

Communist State = 691[P]

Civil rights and duties = :5[E][2P]

Synthesis

W + 691 + :5 = W691:5

As per rule V32 (P1.115) if a document deals any aspect of Politics or History in relation to a particular community or geographical area, it should go under (MC) V History. On the other hand if any aspect of Politics or History deals in a theoretical manner, not confining to any community it should go under the (MC) W Political Science.

4. General Election in India 1997

Analysis

History = V (MC)

India = 44 [P]

Elections = :91[E][2P]

1997 = 'N97 [T]

Synthesis

V + 44:91 + 'N97 = V44:91'N97

5. An introduction to elections in democratic countries

Analysis

Political Science = W (MC)

Democracy = 6 [P]

Elections = :91[E][2P]

Synthesis

W + 6 + :91 = W6:91

6. Constitution of USA

Analysis

History = V (MC)

USA = 73[P]

Constitution = :2[E][2P]

Synthesis

V + 73 + :2 = V73:2

7. Introduction to federal constitutions

Analysis

Political Science = W (MC)

Constitutions = :2[E][2P]

Synthesis

W + :2 = W:2

8. Political parties in democracy

Analysis

Political Science = (MC)

Democracy = 6[P]

Parties = 4,[P2]

Synthesis

W + 6 + ,4 = W6,4

9. International Relations in Changing World

Analysis

Political Science = W (MC)

International relations = :19 [E][2P]

Synthesis

W + :19 = W:19

10. Refugees and International Relations.

Analysis

Political Science = W(MC)

Internation Relations = :19[E][2P]

Intrafacet General relations = Oj

Refugees = 4[E][2P]

Synthesis

W +n :19 + Oj + 4 = W:190j4

Self CheckExercise-5

(a) Introduction to Monarchy

(b) Role of Executive in Communist State

(c) Liberty in Modern State

(d) Unicameralism and Bicameralism

(e) Political Philosophy

(f) The Political Classics

(g) Karl Marx (1818): His life and environment

(h) Electoral Politics

(i) Journal of Refugee studies (UK), 1958

(j) Rousscau on International Relations

11.7 X ECONOMICS

"A Social Science concerned chiefly with description and analysis of the production, distribution and consumption of goods and services''. The facet formula for X Economics is as follows:

X[P]:[E][2P]

Where foci in[P] = Business

Where foci in [E] [2P] = Problem

The following are worked out examples:

1. Indian Banking in 1990's

Analysis

Economics = X (MC)

Bank = 62[P]

India = 44[S]

1990's = 'N9[T]

Synthesis

X + 62 + 44+ 'N9 = X62.44'N9

2. Rate of interest in Commercial Banks

Analysis

Economics = X (MC)

Commercial Bank = 625[P]

Rate of Interest = :11[E] [2P] For 62 Bank in [P] (P2.114)

Synthesis

X + 625 + :11 = X625:11

3. Incidence of Income Tax

Analysis

Economics = XC)

Income Tax = 724 [P]

Incidence = :1[E][2P] For 72 Taxation in [P] (P2.114)

Synthesis

X +724 + :1 = X724:1

4. Devaluation of Indian Currency

Analysis

Economics = X (MC)

Money = 61[P]

Paper currency = :4[M] For 61 Money in [P]

Devaluation = :742 [E][2P]

India = .44[S]

Synthesis

X +61 + ;4 + :742 + .44 = X61;4:742.44

5. Functions of Life Insurance Corporation of India

Analysis

Economics = X (MC)

Life Insurance = 813 [P]

India = .44[S]

Commercial body = ,k (PCI-Personality)

LIC = ,9N5 By (CD)

Functions = :3 [E] Taken from [E] of V History

Synthesis

X + 813 + .44 + ,k + ,9N5 + :3 = X813.44,k9N5:3

6. Cotton textiles industry in India

Analysis

Economics = X(MC)

Cotton Textile Industry= 8(M7;1)[P]

India = .44[S]

Synthesis

X + 8(M7;1)+.44 = X8(M7;1).44

7. Export of Steel products from India during 1990's

Analysis

Economics	= X (MC)
Steel products	= 8 (F1823) [P]
Export	= :545[E][2P]
India	= .44[S]
1990's	= 'N9[T]

Synthesis

X + 8 (F1823) + :545+.44 + 'N9 = X8(F1823):545.44'N9

8. Investigation of accounts of British Iron industry in 1990's

Analysis

Economics	= X(MC)
Iron Industry	= 8(F183) [P]
Accounts	= :8F[E][2P]
Britain	= .56[S]
1990's	= 'N9
Investigation	= :f(PCI[E])

Synthesis

X+8(F182)+:8F+.56+ N9+:f = X8 (F182):8F.56 N9:f

Sector Analysis

As per rule X290 (P1.118), the isolates under 9 Personnel Management are arranged in the three sectors:

1. Least concrete sector 1 to 922 (i.e. 91-967)
2. More concrete sector 9A to 99W
3. Still more concrete sector A to R.

If a document covers more than one sector, the (IN) of each sector should be made of level of [2P] after 9 in [E]. The more concrete sector should be made the earlier level. The following are few worked out examples:

9. Wages of unskilled labour

Analysis

Economics = X(MC)

Unskilled Labour = :99 [E] more concrete sector for 9

Wages = 93[2P] least concrete sector for 9

Synthesis

X:99C+93 = X:99C,3

10. Stock ownership of clerical staff

Analysis

Economics = X(MC)

Clerical Staff = :99P[E] more concrete sector for 9

Stock Ownership = ,37 [2P] least concrete sector for 9

Synthesis

X + :99Psychology + ,37 = X:99P,37

11. Recruitment of Refugee clerical Staff

Analysis

Economics = X(MC)

Refugee = :9J4[E] still concrete sector of 9

Clerical staff = ,9P [2P]more concrete sector for 9

Recruitment = ,~~9~~ 52 [2P] least concrete sector for

Synthesis

X+:954+~~9~~9P +,52 = X:954,9P,52

12. Arbitration of Strike of refugees

Analysis

Economics = X(MC)

Refugee = :9J4 [E] still concrete sector of 9

Strike = ,79 D [2P] more concrete sector for 97

Arbitration = ,6 [2P] least concrete sector for 97

Synthesis

X:954 +~~9~~79D + ,~~9~~ ~~7~~6 = X:954,79D,6

13. Arbitration of strike of Refugee clerical staff

Analysis

Economics	=	X(MC)
Refuge	=	:9J4[E] still concrete sector of 9
Clerical	=	,~~9~~9P[2P]more concrete sector for 9
Strike	=	,979D[2P] more concrete sector for 97
Arbitration	=	,976 [2P] least concrete sector for 97

Synthesis

X+:9J4+,~~9~~9P +,979D+ ,~~9~~ ~~7~~6 = X:9J4,9P,79D,6

14. Cooperative small-scale paper industry

Analysis

Cooperation	=	XM (system)
Small Scale	=	X9B (Special)
Paper industry	=	,8(M13) [P]

Synthesis

XM+,9B+,8 (M13) = XM,9B,8(M13)

15. Strikes in Small Scale Paper Industry

Analysis

Small Scale	=	X9B (Special)
Paper Industry	=	,8(M13)[P]
Strike	=	:979[E][2P]

Synthesis

X9B+,8(M13)+:979D = X9B,8(M13):979D

16. Arbitration in the strike of refugee clerical staff in cooperative small scale paper industry in India in 1990's

Analysis

Cooperation	=	XM (System)

Small Scale	=	X9B (Special)
Paper Industry	=	,8(M13) [P]
Refugee	=	:9J4 [E] still concrete sector of 9
Clerical	=	,99 P[2P]more concrete sector for 9
Strike	=	,979D [2P] more concrete sector for 97
Arbitration	=	,976[2P] least concrete sector for 97
India	=	.44 [S]
1990's	=	'N9[T]

Synthesis

XM+, ~~X~~9B+,8(M13)+:~~9~~J4 +,~~9~~9P +,~~9~~79D + ,~~9~~~~7~~6 +.44+'N9 = XM,9B,8(M13):9J4,9P,79D,6.44'N9

Self Check Exercise-6

(a) History of land mortgage banks in India
(b) Cheque system in foreign banks
(c) Management of Life Insurance in India
(d) Exports of Rubber from India
(e) Unskilled labour
(f) Adjudication of grievances of urban clerical staff
(g) Management of large scale cooperative sugar industry
(h) Strike of clerical staff in large scale cooperative sugar industry
(i) A concise economic history of the world
(j) The British Electric Industry 1875-1914
(k) Readings in labour economics
(l) The nature of unemployment in India
(m) Market socialism in Yugoslavia
(n) Productivity and growth in Indian manufacturing
(o) Economic trends in Chinese agriculture

11.8 Y SOCIOLOGY

"The Science of Society, Social institutions and social relationship'' The facet formula for Y Sociology is as follows:

Y[P]:[E][2P]:[2E]:[2E][3P]

Where foci in [P] = Group

Where foci in [E][2P] = Problem

Where foci in [2E][3P] = Secondary Problem

The following are worked out examples:

1. Introduction to family

Analysis

Sociology	= Y(MC)
Family	= 2[P]

Synthesis

Y+2 = Y2

2. Rural Sociology of India

Analysis

Sociology	= Y (MC)
Rural	= 31 [P]
India	= .44 [S]

Synthesis

Y + 31 + .44 = Y31.44

3. Indian anthropology

Analysis

Sociology	= Y(MC)
Anthropology	= 7 [P]
India	= 44 By (GD)

Synthesis

Y + 7 44 = Y744

As per rule Y191 (P1.120) the class Y Sociology may frequently require the application of super imposition Device (SID) in the construction of Group Numbers.

4. Sociology of African Primitive races

Analysis

Sociology	= Y (MC)

Primitive Race = 72[P]

"—" = Connecting symbol for (SID)

Africa = 76

Synthesis

Y + 72 + -+76 = Y72-76

5. Pre-historic races of India

Analysis

Sociology = Y(MC)

Prehistoric race = 71[P]

"—" Connecting symbol for (SID)

India = 744 [P]

Synthesis

Y+71+-+744 = Y71-744

6. Culture and civilization of China

Analysis

Sociology = Y(MC)

Civilization, Culture = 1[E] [2P]

China = .41 [S]

Synthesis

Y+:1.41 = Y:1.41

7. Marriage customs of Hindus

Analysis

Sociology = Y(MC)

Hindus = 73 (Q2) [P]

Activity = :3[E] To be divided as [P] of R4 Ethics

Marriage = 217 To be taken from [P] of R4 Ethics

Synthesis

Y+73(Q2)+:3+217 = Y73 (Q2):3217

8. Chamole Earthquake relief work

Analysis

Sociology = Y(MC)

Earthquake = :436[E][2P]

Relief work = :67[2E] [3P]

Chamole = .4452 CH

Synthesis

Y+:436+:67+.4452CH = Y:436:67.4452CH

9. Prohibition through legislation in Andhra Pradesh

Analysis

Sociology = Y(MC)

Alcoholism = :411[E][2P]

Prevention through legislation = :5(Z)

Andhra Pradesh = .4416

Synthesis

Y+:411+:5(Z)+.4416 = Y:411:5(Z).4416

10. Intelligence of American Race

Analysis

Sociology = Y (MC)

American Race = 773 [P]

Personality = :7 [E][2P] To be as in S Psychology

Intelligence = 72 Taken from [E] [2P] of S Psychology

Synthesis

Y+773+:7+2 = Y7732:72

11. The aboriginals of Asia and their agriculture implements

Analysis

Sociology = Y (MC)

Aboriginals = 72 [P]

Asia = -74 By (SID)

Agricultural Implements = :83 (J) [E] [2P]

Synthesis

Y+72+-74+:83(J) – Y72-74:83(J)

12. Gold Ear rings for Muslim Women

Sociology	=	Y(MC)
Women	=	15 [P]
Muslim	=	-73 (Q7) To be got by (SID)
Ear rings	=	:8683 [E][2P]
Gold	=	; (E118) To be got by (SD)

Synthesis

Y+15+-73(Q7)+:8683+;(E118) = Y15-73(Q7):8683;(E118)

13. Community Development programmes in India

Sociology	=	Y(MC)
Rural	=	15[P]
Personality	=	:7[E][2P]
Development	=	:7[2E] [3P]
India	=	.44

Synthesis

Y+15+:7+:7+.44 = Y15:7:7:7.44

14. Convergent issue in Demography and Genetics

Analysis

Sociology	=	Y (MC)
Demography	=	:5[E][2P]
Oa		General Phase Relation
Genetics	=	G:6

Synthesis

Y+:5+Oa+G:6 = Y:5OaG:6

15 Communities, Riots and Survivors in South Asia

Analysis

Sociology	=	Y (MC)
Urban	=	33[P]
Crime	=	:45 [E] [2P]

South Asia = .49 (19G) [S]

Synthesis

Y+33+:45+,49G = Y33:45.49G

Self Check Exercise-7

(a) Sociology of Marriage

(b) Sociology of Aryan rece

(c) Gandhiji's views on Prohibition

(d) Psychology of murder

(e) Charity for the war Victims of Kosavo in 1999

(f) An introduction to Ornaments of Hindu community

(g) Tattooing among the women of Coastal Districts of Andhra Pradesh

(h) The evolution of Women's Asylums in 1500 A.D.

(i) Race and Slavery in the Middle-East

(j) A study of Portuguese fishing community

(k) The manners and customs of the Chinese

(l) Civilization of Black Africa

11.9 Z LAW

"A rule of conduct or action prescribed or formally recognized as binding or enforced by a controlling authority''. The facet formula for Z Law is as follows:

Z[P],[P2],[P3],[P4]

Where foci in [P] = Community To be got by (GD) and (SD)

Where foci in [P2] = Law I

Where foci in [P3] = Law II

Where foci in [P4] = For 7 judgment and decree in [P3]

The following are worked out examples

1. Indian Law

Analysis

Law = Z (MC)

India = 44[P] To be got by (GD)

Synthesis

Z + 44 = Z 44

2. Hindu Law

Analysis

Law = Z (MC)

Hindu = (Q2) [P] To be got by (SD)

Synthesis

Z + (Q2) = Z(Q2)

3. Indian Laws relating to landlord and tenant

Analysis

Law = Z (MC)

India = 44[P] To be got by (GD)

Land = ,211[P2]

Land Lord and Tenant = ,3[P3]

Synthesis

Z + 44 + 211 ++ ,3 = Z44,211,3

4. Muslim law of succession

Analysis

Law = Z (MC)

Muslim community = (Q7) [P] To be got by (SD()

Property = ,2[P2]

Succession = ,6 [P3]

Synthesis

Z+(Q7)+,2+,6 = Z(Q7),2,6

5. Cases and materials on International Law

Analysis

Law = Z(MC)

International = 1[P] To be got by (GD)

Case Study = y7 (ACI-Applicable before Space Facet)

Synthesis

Z+1+y7 = Z1y7

6. Indian Supreme Court Digest, 1998

Analysis

Law = Z (MC)

India = 44[P] To be got by (GD)

Supreme Court = ,81 [P2]

Digest = y8 (ACI-Applicable before Space Facet)

1998 = N98

Synthesis

Z+44+,81+y8+N98 = Z44,81y8N98

7. Biography of M.C. Setalvad (1901)

Analysis[2P]

Law = Z(MC)

India = 44[P] To be got by (GD)

Court = ,8[P2]

Attorney General = ,51 [P3]

Biography = w (ACI- Applicable before Space Facet)

M.C.Setalvad = N01 [P] To be got by (CD)

Synthesis

Z+44,8+,51+w+N01 = Z44,8,51wN01

8. Bombay Registration Manual

Analysis

Law = Z (MC)

Bombay = 4431 [P] To be got by (GD)

Document = ,98 [P2]

Registration = :3 Foci in [E] [2P] for 98 document in [P2]

Synthesis

Z+4431+,98+:3 = Z4431,98:3

9. Indian laws relating to Naval War

Analysis

Law = Z (MC)

India = 44[P] To be got by (GD)

Naval war = ,C [p2]

Synthesis

Z+44+,C = Z44,C

10. International Laws relating to prisoner of war

Analysis

Law = Z(MC)

International = 1[P] To be got by (GD)

War = ,A [P2]

Prisoners of war = 6, [P3]

Synthesis

Z+1+,A+,6 = Z1,A,6

11. Year Book of European Law, OUP 1991

Analysis

Law = Z(MC)

Europe = 5[P] To beg to by (GD)

Year Book = n (ACI-Applicable before Space Facet)

UK = 56 [P] To be got by (GD)

1991 = ,N91 [P2] To be got by (GD)

Synthesis

Z+5+n+56+,N91 = Z5n56,N91

12. A Legal History of Trade Unionism 1721-1906

Analysis

Law = Z (MC)

Trade Unionism = (X:97D) [P] To be got by (SD)

History = v (ACI-Applicable before Space Facet)

1721-1906 = 'L21 → 'N06

Synthesis

Z+(X:7D)+v+'L21 → N06 = Z(X:97D)v'L21 → 'N06

Self Check Exercise

(a) Muslim Law

(b) Hindu Law of will

(c) British Law of fraud and mistakes

(d) Christian Law relating to succession of adopted child

(e) Laws relating to declaration of war

(f) The law of contract in Malaysia

(g) Treatment of Prisoners under International law

(h) International Journal of Refugee Law, 1991

(i) Crime and Computer

(j) Torts in New Zealand

(k) Laws relating ownership of property in China

11.10 SUMMARY

In the preceeding sections we have introduced you to the art and technique of classifying titles under Social Sciences. The (MCs) under Social Sciences are: S Psychology, T Education, U Geography, V History, W Political Sciences, X Economics, Y Sociology and Z Law. The facet formula provided for each of the (MCs) are explained and well demonstrated by worked out examples. The relevant rules from Part I of CC have been cited to articulate the intricacies in the construction of Class Number or Number Building. The occurrence of each facet in a given title has been analysed citing the relevant focal numbers from the schedules and synthesized to arrive at co-extensive class number. Through self-check exercises provided for under each (MC), you will have ample opportunity for classifying documents with CC. This practice would keep you in good stead to apply various rules and techniques of Classification presented in part I of CC.

11.11 ANSWERS TO SELF-CHECK EXERCISES

Exercises-1

(a) S4(2),

(b) S758

(c) S55:524

(d) S;7

(e) S25:24:2

(f) SM9,51:52

(g) S : (Δ :36)

(h) SN1:f

(i) SM : f

(j) S : (T) : f

Exercise-2

(a) T9(Y394),44

(b) T:2(B2)

(c) T15:3.,1

(d) T4:3(2),97

(e) T4:3(P5)

(f) T4:4,2

(g) TN1:3

(h) TN3,2:3(B2),144'N6

(i) T9(Y4):8.44

(j) T4.4416,e,9N18v

(k) T.44'N66t

(*l*) T48,n44,n44,N69S

Exercise –3

(a) U21OaJ:1

(b) U(X:8(A))56"M

(c) U.44.g7H

(d) Uf43

(e) U.44Q7

(f) U8urM72

Exercise-4

(a) V44,31

(b) V44,21:3

(c) V58:1956
(d) V44y7M86
(e) V(R)
(f) Vnl,N92
(g) V1
(h) V44:1941(Y:1)
(i) V44:76'N97
(j) V4437:72

Exercise-5

(a) W4
(b) W691,2
(c) W:11,
(d) W,3
(e) WL(R)
(f) Wx
(g) W691wM18
(h) W:91
(i) W:44m56,N58
(j) W:19xL12

Exercise-6

(a) X6261v44
(b) X6295:5
(c) X813:8.44
(d) X8(J711):545.44
(e) X:99C
(f) X:945,9Psychology,79B,7
(g) XM,9D,8(J94):8
(h) XM,9D,8(J94):99P,79D
(i) Xvl
(j) X8(D66).56'M75→'N14

(k) X:9

(l) X:9911.44

(m) XM2:51.5923

(n) X8(A):2

(o) X8(5).41

Exercise-7

(a) Y217

(b) Y73(P1)

(c) Y:411:5

(d) Y:45112

(e) Y:438:68.5923knowledge'N99

(f) Y15-73(Q2):86

(g) Y15-744158:8697

(h) Y15:4:65 -'J

(i) Y7:451262.46

(j) Y9(MY65).542

(k) Y741:356

(l) Y76:1S

Exercise-8

(a) Z(Q7)

(b) Z(Q2),2,41

(c) Z456,555

(d) Z(Q6),1236,6

(e) Z,A,1

(f) ZLG)

(g) Z435,3

(h) Z1,A6

(i) Z,135m1,N91

(j) Z5OaD6,8(B)

(k) Z937,4

(l) Z41,2,1

11.12 ASSIGNMENT

Assign Class Number to the following Titles:

1. What is an Emotion
2. The Metaphysics of Mind
3. Education in France 1848-1870
4. An introduction to Adult Education
5. The University in Society
6. Mathematics for Geographers
7. Early Maps of South East Asia
8. The Philosophy of History
9. Annie Besant, a biography
10. Jawaharlala Nehru, the Centenary Volume
11. Parliamentary versus Presidential Government
12. British Policy towards Ireland, 1921-1941
13. Parliamentary privilege in India
14. An introduction to Econometrics
15. Readings in Labour Economics
16. The Bombay Textile strike, 1982-1983
17. A History of British Trade Unionism since 1889
18. The Psychology of Finance
19. Evaluating Social Science Research in India
20. The Psychology of the Chinese People
21. Home care for older people in Europe
22. Drugs and Drug control in USA
23. An introduction to Islamic Law
24. The international Law of the Sea
25. An introduction to law of contract

UNIT 12

Other Main Classes: Generalia, Library Science, Useful Arts And Spiritual Experience and Mysticism

12.0 OBJECTIVES

In Unit 11, we have introduced you to the art of classification of titles under Social Sciences. In this unit, we will introduce you to the classification of titles under the (MCs) Generalia, Library Science, Useful Arts, and Spiritual Experience and Mysticism. After going through this unit you should be able to:

- Understand the rules of classification of each of the (MCs)
- Know the facet formula of each of (MC) and its implications, and
- Assign class numbers to titles falling the (MCs) Generalia, Library Science, Useful Arts and Spiritual Experience and Mysticism

12.1 INTRODUCTION

In Unit 11, we have introduced you to classify documents under Social Sciences. In this unit we will introduce you to classify documents falling under a Generalia, 2 Library Science, M Useful Arts and Δ Spiritual Experience and Mysticism. Each (MC) will be introduced to you citing its facets formula, explaining the implications of each facet and relevant and important rules stated in Part I of CC and well supported by worked out examples. Let us take up each one of these (MCs)

12.2 z GENERALIA: RULES

If any publication deals with several subjects and which cannot be put under any single (MC) listed in chapter 1 of the schedules (P2.4), then we have to put that publications under Generalia Main Class. Small z is used to represent Zeneralia.

As per rule 9z2 (P1.62) if the exposition is confined only to generalia materials on a, specific geographical area the digit z should be divided by (GD) using the area concerned. Here are few examples.

Indology z44 → India (GD)

Sinology z41 → China (GD)

Orientology z4 → Asia (GD)

Americana z7 → North America (GD)

As per rule 9z3 "if the exposition is confined only to generalia materials by and on a specific person, the digit z should be amplified by (AD) using the name of the person".

Gandhiana zG → First letter of Gandhi

Nehruana zN → First letter of Nehru

Lincolniana zL → First letter of Lincoln

As per rule 9z4 of the digit z is not amplified by (GD) or (AD) and calls for the use of (ACI), the digit z may be omitted and it is sufficient if the Class Number begins with (ACI) digit. Here are few examples

Encyclopedia Britannica	k56,L	but not zk56,L
Encyclopedia Americana	k73,M	but not zk73,M
India Today	m44,N7	but not zm44,N7
Readers Digest	m1,M50	but not zm1,M50
World of Learning, 1947	m1,N4	but not zn1,N4

12.3 a GENERALIA BIBLIOGRAPHY

The facet formula for a Generalia Bibliogrpahy is as follows.

a[P], [P2] [P3], [P4]

Where foci in [P] = Material

Where foci in [P2] = Kind

When (IN) in [P2] is 1 i.e. list publications in geographical area
[P3] is Area Tobe got by (CD)
[T] is period (LED)

When (IN) in [P2] is 2 i.e. Library Catalogue
[P3] is Country to be got b (GD)
[P4] is Origin to be got by (CD)

When (IN) is Union Catalogue

[P3] is Geographical Area covered to be got by (GD)

When (IN) in [P2] is 3 or 4 i.e. Publishers Catalogue and Book Sellers Catalogue [P3] is Publishers or Book Seller to be got by (AD)

When (IN) in [P2] is 5 i.e. catalogue of exhibition
[P3] is Country to be got by (GD)
[P4] is Origin to be got by (CD)

The foci in [P3] and [P4] depends upon the isolates given in [P2]. The table of facet formula is given at page 1.63. Here are few worked out examples.

1. Bibliography of Manuscripts

   Analysis

   Bibliography = a (MC)

   Manuscript = 12 [P]

   Synthesis

   a + 12 = a12

2. Bibliography of Sanskrit Manuscripts

   Analysis

   Bibliography = a (MC)

   Manuscripts = 12[P]

   Sanskrit = 15 [P]

Both the isolates are from the same facet i.e [P]. We have to are super imposition device (SID). See P1.33 for SID

Synthesis

A + 12 + - + 15 = a12 – 15

3. Bibliography of French Newspapers

Analysis

Bibliography = a (MC)

Newspapers = 44 [P]

(SID) = "–"

Language = 3 [P] to be divided by Language

French = 122 (Taken from Language Isolates)

Analysis

A + 44 + - + 3 + 122 = a 44-3122

4. Bibliography of Persian Translations in to Hindi

Analysis

Bibliography = a (MC)

Translation = 95 [P]

As per instructions in the schedules (P2.29) 95 is to be divided first by the language of the original and the language of the translation. A hyphen should be inserted between the two language numbers

Persian 164
Hindi 152] = Taken from Language Isolates P2.26

Synthesis

A + 95 + 164 + - 152 = a95164 – 152

5. Indian National Bibliography (1958)

Analysis

Bibliography = a (MC)

Book (Conventional) = 43 [P]

List of Publications in a geographical area = 1 [P2]

India (Area) = 44 [P3]

1958 = N5 [T](LED)

Synthesis

a + 43 + 1 + 44 + 'N5 = a43, 144'N5

6. Books in Print 1948 (Annual)

Analysis

Bibliography = a(MC)

Book = 43 [P]

List of Publications in a geographical area = 1 [P2]

USA (area) = 73 [P3]

1948 = N4 [T] (LED)

Synthesis

A+43+1+73+'N4=a43,173'N4

NOTE: This is an annual publication. If this aspect is to be represented, the class number shall be a43,173n73,N4

7. Reference Catalogue of Current Literature (1874)

Analysis

Bibliography = a (MC)

Book (Conventional) = 43 [P]

List of publications in a geographical area = ,1[P2]

Great Britain (Area) = 56 [P3] to be got by (GD)

1874 = 'M7 [T] (LED)

Synthesis

A + 43 + ,1 + 56 + 'M7 – a43, 156 'M7

8. Osmania University Library Catalogue of Persian Manuscripts (1960)

Analysis

Bibliography = a(MC)

Manuscripts = 12 [P]

By Language = 3 [P]

NOTE: Both isolates have been taken from the same facet i.e. [P]. These two isolates have to be brought together by using – (SID)

Persian Language = 164 the digit 3 is to further divided by language

Library Catalogue = ,2[P2]

Country (India) = 44 [P3] Tobe got by [GD]

1960 (Origin) = ,N60 [P3] Tobe got by (CD)

Synthesis

A + 12 + - + 3 + 164 + ,2 + 44 + , N60 = a 12 – 3164,244,N60

9. Union Catalogue of Learned Periodicals in South Asia

Analysis

Bibliography = a (MC)

Periodical = 46[P]

List of publications in a geographical area = ,1[P2]

South Asia (Area Covered) = 43 [P3] to be got by (GD)

Synthesis

A + 46 + ,1 + 43 = a46,143

10. Monthly List Sage Publications India (P) Ltd

Analysis

Bibliography = a(MC)

Book (Conventional) = 43 [P]

Publishers Catalogue = ,3 [P2]

Publisher (Sage) = S[P3] to be got by (AD)

Synthesis

A+43+,3+S = a43, 3S

Self Check Exercise-1

(a) Bibliography of News Papers

(b) Bibliography of Sanskrit translations in to English

(c) Bibliography of Periodicals for women

(d) British National Bibliography (1950)

(e) British National Catalogue of Periodicals

(f) Bibliography of English books on International Affairs

(g) Catalogue of Telugu Manuscripts in Tanjore Saraswati Mahal Library, 1960

(h) T. R. Publications Catalogue, 1997-1998

(i) Indian Books in Print, 1998

(j) British Scientific and Technical Books, 1953-57

(k) Biography of Sir William Jones (1746-1794)

12.4 2 LIBRARY SCIENCE

The facet formula for 2 Library Science is as follows

2[P];[M]:[E][2P]

Where foci in [P] = Type of Library

Where foci in [M] = Material to be got from [P] of a Gineralia Bibliography

Where foci in [E] [2P] = Problem

The following are few worked out examples

1. Public Libraries in India

Analysis

Library Science = 2 (MC)

Public Library = 2 [P]

India = .44[S]

Synthesis

2 + 2 + .44 = 22.44

2. Lending of Periodicals in the University Library

Analysis

Library Science = 2 (MC)

University Library = 34[P]

Periodicals = ;46[M] to be got from [P] if generalia Bibliography

Lending = :62[E][2P]

Synthesis

2 + 34 + ;46 + :62 = 234; 46 : 62

3. Cataloguing of Books in Agricultural Library

Analysis

Library Science = 2 (MC)

Business Library = 4[P] other by (SD)

Agriculture = (J) to be got by (SD)

Books = ;43 [M] to be got from [P] of a Generalia Bibliography

Cataloguing = :55[E][2P]

Synthesis

2 + 4 + (J) + ;43 + :55 = 24 (J);43:55

4. Classification of Patents in Commence Library By CC

Analysis

Library Science = 2 [MC]

Commence Library = 45 [P]

Patents = ;45 [M] to be got from [P] of a Generalia Bibliography

CC = :51N3

NOTE: (See P1.64 for ready made class numbers for some important classification schemes)

Synthesis

2 + 45 ;45 + :51N3 = 245;45:51N3

5. Classified Catalogue Code (CCC)

NOTE: As per rule 92355 (P1.64) a specific catalogue code should be individual by (CD)

Analysis

Library Science = 2 (MC)

Cataloguing = :55[E] [2P]

CCC = N3 to be got by (CD) (First edition was published in 1934)

Synthesis

2 + :55 + N3 = 2 : 55 N3

6. Classification of Physics By UDC

NOTE: As per rule 924 (P1.64) when the focus in [E] is classification [2P] may subject classified and its number should be got by (SD)

Analysis

Library Science = 2 (MC)

UDC = :51M96 [E] (see P1.64 for readymade number)

Physics = (C) [2P] to be got by (SD)

Synthesis

2+:51M96+(C) = 2:51M96(C)

7. Annals of Library Science And Documentation, 1992

Analysis

Library Science = 2 (MC)

Periodical = m (ACI =- Applicable before Space Facet)

India = 44 [P]to be got by (GD)

1992 = ,N92 [P2] to be got by (CD)

Synthesis

2+m+44+,N92 = 2m44,N92

8. Indian National Scientific Documentation Centre (Estd. 1952)

Analysis

Library Science = 2 (MC)

Documentation = :97 [E] [2P]

India = .44 [S]

Institution = ,d (PCI-Personality Common Isolate)

1952 = ,9N52 to be got by (CD) (See rule 271 at page 20 in the annexure)

Synthesis

2 + :97 + .44 + ,d + ,9N52 = 2:97.44,d,9N52

9. Biography of Melvil Dewey (1851-1931)

Analysis

Library Science = 2 (MC)

Classification = :51[E][2P]

Biography = w (ACI-Application before Space Facet)

Dewey (1851) = M51[P] to be got by (CD)

Synthesis

2 + :51 + w + M51 = 2:51 wM51

10. Collected works of S.R. Ranganathan (1892-1972)

Analysis

Library Science = 2 (MC)

Collected Works = x (ACI – Applicable before Space Facet)

Ranganathan (1892) = M92 [P] to be got by (CD)

Synthesis

2+x+M92 = 2xM92

Self-Check Exercise-2

(a) Maintenance of gramophone records in the libraries for the visually handicapped

(b) AACR-Cataloguing Rules 1967

(c) Cooperation of National Libraries of the world

(d) Classification of Religion according to DDC

(e) Herald of Library Science, Lucknow, 1997

(f) A Librarian looks back: autobiography of SR. Ranganathan (1892-1972)

(g) Encyclopedia of Library and Information Science, New York, Marcel Dekkar, 1997

(h) Report on International Conference on Cataloguing Principles, Paris, 1961

(i) A guide to Library Research Methods

(j) Academic Libraries: Role in the National Development

12.5 M USEFUL ARTS

Ranganathan has rightly pointed out it is a miscellaneous class or a hold all class. This class accommodates all the arts and crafts, in fact all the application sciences not provided in the (MCs). This (MC) is further divided on canonical lines. Most of these canonical classes (CNCs) are gaining, of late, literary warrant, But the schedules is only brief and may not meet the requirement of present day needs of Libraries and Information Centres. For some of the canonical divisions like M7 Textiles and MJ7 we find facet formula and shorter schedule.

12.5.1 Canonical Divisions

The Important Canonical Divisions are:

M1 Book production and description

M3 Domestic Science

M7 Textiles

M8 Dress Making

MJ7 Rope making

MY1 Physical Training

MY2 Athletics

MY3 Indoor amusement games

MY4 Animal Racing

MY6 Hunting

12.5.2 M7 Textiles

The facet formula for M7 Textiles is as follows:

M7[P];[M]:[E][2P]

NOTE: The above is revised facet formula and schedule provided for M7 Textiles in the annexure at page 27.

Where foci in [P] = Product

Where foci in [M] = Material

Where foci in [E] [2P] = Work

The following are few worked out examples:

1. Cotton textiles

   Analysis

   Textiles = M7 (CNC)

   Cotton = ; 1[M]

   Synthesis

   M7 +;1 = M7 ; 1

2. Bleaching in Cotton textiles

Analysis

Textiles = M7 (CNC)

Cotton =; 1[M]

Bleaching = :5[E]

Synthesis

M7 + ;7:5 = M7;1:5

5. Washing Silk Textiles

Analysis

Textiles = M7 (CNC)

Silk = ;3[M]

Washing = :7[E]

Synthesis

M7 +;3 + :7 = M7;3:7

3. Woolen Carpet Knitting

Analysis

Textiles = M7 (CNC)

Carpet = 5 [P]

Wool = ;2 [M]

Knitting = :4 [E]

Synthesis

M7 + 5 + ;2 +:4 = M75;2:4

4. Twisting Metal Yarn

Analysis

Textiles = M7 (CNC0

Yarn = 1 [P]

Metal = ;998 [M]

Twisting = :2[E]

Synthesis

M7 + 1 +;998 + :2 = M71;998:2

12.5.3 MJ7 Rope Making

The facet formula for MJ7 Rope Making is as follows:

MJ7[P] : [E] [2P]

Where foci in [P] = Material

Where foci in [E] [2P] = Work, Same as in M7 Textiles

The following are worked out examples

1. Coir Ropes

Analysis

Rope Making = MJ7 (CNC)

Coir = 2 [P]

Synthesis

MJ7 + 2 = MJ72

2. Cotton rope Carding

Analysis

Rope Making = MJ7 (CNC)

Cotton = 1 [P]

Carding = :5 [E] (From foci in [E] of M7 Textiles. See Annexure P27)

Synthesis

MJ7 + 1 +:5 = MJ71:5

3. Twisting Jute Ropes

Analysis

Rope Making = MJ7 (CNC)

Jute = 5 [P]

Twisting = :2[E] (From foci in [E] of M7 Textiles. See annexure P27)

Synthesis

MJ7 + 5 + :2 = MJ75 : 2

4. Dyeing vegetable fibre

Analysis

Rope Making = MJ7 (CNC)

Vegetable fibre = 97 [P]

Dyeing = :8 [E] (From foci in [E] of M7 Textiles. See annexure P27)

Synthesis

MJ7 + 97 + :8 = MJ 797 : 8

5. Sizing Metal Ropes

Analysis

Rope Making = MJ7 (CNC)

Metal = 98 [P]

Sizing = :6 [E] (From foci in [E] of M7 textiles. See annexure P27)

Synthesis

MJ7 + 98 + :6 = MJ798 : 6

12.5.4 Examples From other Canonical Classes

1. Beauty Culture, MA7
2. Journal of Printing Published form Chennai, 1999 M143m44,N99
3. Biography of Viswanathan Anand (1969) MY322 M69
4. 'Wisden'the Cricket Almanac, 1999 MY2141n42,N99
5. Introduction to Horology MB9
6. International Philately Congress held at New Delhi, 1998 MYX46pl, N98
7. Invisible light, Photography in Australia M95.8
8. Life of Jim Corbet MY6WM80
9. Sports and the British: A modern history MYv56'N
10. Biography of Wilson Jones (1922) MY33 w N22

Self Check Exercise –3

(a) The English Cotton Industry and World Market, 1815-1896

(b) Indian Diary and Album

(c) The Oxford Guide to World Games, 1984

(d) Baseball, the peoples game

(e) The love of cycling

(f) China Races

(g) Man Eater of Kumaon

(h) An A-Z of sailing terms

(i) Biography of Michael Jordan (1963)

(j) The Board of Control for Cricket in India

12.6. Δ SPIRITUAL EXPERIENCE AND MYSTICISM

This Main class is special in nature and did not find in any printed scheme of classification except CC. Since Arabic numbers and Roman Alphabets had already been exhausted to represent other (MCs), Ranganathan introduced a new symbol Δ which represents mystical significance and hence chosen to represent Spiritual Experience and Mysticism. There is a lengthy explanation of this (MC) in theory part of CC (Pl1-92 to 1.93). The facet formula for the (MC), Δ Spiritual Experience and Mysticism is as follows:

Δ [P], [P2]:[E] [2P]

Where foci in [P] = Religion

Where foci in [P2] = Entity

Where foci in [E] [2P] = Problem

The following are worked out examples.

1. Hindu Mysticism

Analysis

Spiritual Experience and Mysticism = Δ(MC)

Hindu Religion = 2 [P]

Synthesis

Δ + 2 = Δ 2

2. Breath Control in Raja Yoga

Analysis

Spiritual Experience and Mysticism = Δ (MC)

Raja Yoga = 26 [P]

Breath Control = :34 [E] [2P]

Synthesis

Δ + 26 + :34 = Δ 26:34

3. Buddhist Meditation

Analysis

Spiritual Experience and Mysticism = Δ (MC)

Budhistic religion = 4 [P]

Meditation = :36 [E] [2P]

Synthesis

Δ + 4 + :36 = Δ 4: 36

4. Vision of God

Analysis

Spiritual Experience and Mysticism = Δ (MC)

God = , 11[P2]

Vision = :5 [E][2P]

Synthesis

Δ + ;11 + :5 = Δ 11:5

5. Peter Vidal:What 1984 Holds for You

Analysis

Spiritual Experience and Mysticism = Δ (MC)

Astrology = :864 [E][2P]

Synthesis

Δ + :864 = Δ :864

6. Astrological Magazine, Bangalore, 1997

Analysis

Spiritual Experience and Mysticism = Δ (MC)

Astrology = :864

Periodical = m (ACI-Applicable before Space)

India = 44 [P] to be got by (CD)

1997 = ,N97[P] to be got by (CD)

Synthesis

Δ + :864 + m + 44 + ,N97 = Δ :864m44,N97

7. Biography of PC Sorkar (1920)

As per rule Δ 9Y7 (P1.94), the (ACI) Number for the lives of Mystics and realized persons is y7 and not w

Analysis

Spiritual Experience and Mysticism = Δ (MC)

Magic =:87 [E] [2P]

Biography (Case study) = y7 (ACI)

P.C. Sorkar (1920) = N20[P] to be got by (CD)

Synthesis

Δ + :87 + y7 + N20 = Δ:87 y7N20

8. Mystical Exposition of Chemistry

As per rule Δ 86 (P1.94) Δ should be amplified by (SD) to represent mystical or occult exposition of subjects excepts Fine Arts, Literature and Religion.

Analysis

Mysticism = Δ (MC)

Chemistry = (E) To be got by (SD)

Synthesis

Δ+ (E) = Δ (E)

9. Occult Exposition of Civilization

Analysis

Mysticism = Δ (MC)

Civilization = (Y:1) To be got by (SD)

Synthesis

Δ + (Y:1) = Δ (Y:1)

10. Planets in Hindu Astrology

Analysis

Spiritual Experience and Mysticism = Δ (MC)

Hindu = 2[P]

Nature = ,2[P2] to be divided as in [P3] of ND sculpture

Planets = 84

Astrology = 864 [E][2P]

Synthesis

Δ + 2+ , 2 + 84 +:864 + Δ 2,284:864

Self Check Exercise-4

(a) The Saints of Kaveri Delta

(b) Biography of Yogi Vemana 1550-1650)

(c) Africa in the grip of witch craft during 19th century
(d) Indian rope walking
(e) Practical palmistry
(f) Practice of Hatha yoga
(g) Propehcy in Christianity
(h) Omens in respect of water in Islam
(i) Vision of disembodied souls
(j) Mystic manifestation of women diseases

12.7 SUMMARY

In the proceedings sections we have introduced you to the art and technique of classifying titles under the (MCs) a Generalia Bibliography, 2 Library Science M useful Arts and Δ Spiritual Experience and Mysticism. The facet formula provided for each of the (MCs) are explained and well demonstrated by worked out examples. The relevant rules from part I of CC have been cited to articulate the intricacies in the construction of Class Number. The occurrence of each facet in a given title has been analysed citing relevant focal numbers from the schedules and synthesized to arrive at coextensive Class Number. Through self-check exercises provided for under each (MC) you have ample opportunity for classifying documents with CC. This practice would keep you in good stead to apply various rules and techniques of classification presented in part I of CC.

12.8 ANSWERS TO SELF-CHECK EXERCISES

Exercise-1

(a) a44,
(b) a9515-111
(c) a46-815
(d) a43,156'N5
(e) a46,156
(f) W:19a43-311
(g) a12-335,244N60

(h) a43,3TRP

(i) a43,144'N98

(j) Aa43,156'N53→N57

(k) zGwL46

Exercise-2

(a) 268;13:88

(b) 2:55N6

(c) 213:4m1

(d) 2:51MQ

(e) 2m44,N97

(f) 2:51wM92,1

(g) 2k73,N97

(h) 2:55p1,N61

(i) 2:f

(j) 230bX:89ZB,44

Exericise-3

(a) M7;1v56'M15 → M96

(b) M95.44

(c) MY.1

(d) MY31k56,N91

(e) MY322

(f) MY2142.73

(g) MY266

(h) MY5.41

(i) MY6.445

(j) MY251P111)

(k) MY2wN63

(l) MY2141.44,b,9N5

Execise-4

(a) Δ 2y7x.441.e5k

(b) Δ 2y7j50

(c) Δ :87.6'M

(d) Δ :87.44

(e) Δ :8627

(f) Δ 22

(g) Δ 6:86

(h) Δ 7,25:9692

(i) Δ ,16:5

(j) Δ (L9F:4):83

12.9 ASSIGNMENT

1. Catalogue of Arabic Manuscripts in Raza Library, Rampur
2. A Survey of work done on Military History of India
3. Trying to be in tune with Krishna Murthi (1865), this is my life
4. Cooking Delights
5. Seminar on planning for increasing India's Book Exports, New Delhi, 1996
6. The Planning of Library and Documentation Services
7. Mystics and Men of Miracles in India
8. Secrets of Natural Beauty
9. Publishing in India, an analysis
10. Cotton piece dyeing
11. Indian Books in print, a bibliography of Indian Books up to Dec. 1972 in English Language, 3 vols.
12. A Catalogue of Sanskrit Manuscripts in the collection of Asiatic Society
13. Astrology and Jyotirvidya; the fundamental principles
14. National Book Trust (India) Annual Report, 1996
15. The Science of Meditation
16. Household textiles and Laundry work
17. Principles of Basketball
18. Indian Hockey, Extra time or Sudden death
19. Punjab University, Chandigarh: Doctoral Dissertations, 1948-1964
20. Rajasthan University Library: Union Catalogue of Periodicals,1965

Index